FROM WORRY TO WORSHIP

A 52-Week Devotional Bible Study for

Anxiety

A SELF-HELP DEVOTIONAL FOR ANXIETY, WORRY, AND STRESS RELIEF

GRACE ANDREWS

© Copyright 2025 by Grace Andrews

All Rights Reserved

From Worry to Worship

A 52-Week Devotional Bible Study for Anxiety

A Self-Help Devotional for Anxiety, Worry, and Stress Relief

The content contained within this book may not be reproduced, duplicated or transmitted without direct written permission from the author or the publisher.

Under no circumstances will any blame or legal responsibility be held against the publisher, or author, for any damages, reparation, or monetary loss due to the information contained within this book, either directly or indirectly.

Scripture quotations taken from The Holy Bible, New International Version® NIV®

Copyright © 1973, 1978, 1984, 2011 by Biblica, Inc.

Used with permission. All rights reserved worldwide.

Legal Notice:

This book is copyright protected. It is only for personal use. You cannot amend, distribute, sell, use, quote or paraphrase any part, or the content within this book, without the consent of the author or publisher.

Disclaimer Notice:

Please note the information contained within this document is for educational and entertainment purposes only. All effort has been executed to present accurate, up to date, reliable, complete information. No warranties of any kind are declared or implied. Readers acknowledge that the author is not engaged in the rendering of legal, financial, medical or professional advice. The content within this book has been derived from various sources. Please consult a licensed professional before attempting any techniques outlined in this book.

By reading this document, the reader agrees that under no circumstances is the author responsible for any losses, direct or indirect, that are incurred as a result of the use of the information contained within this document, including, but not limited to, errors, omissions, or inaccuracies.

ISBN 978-1-7638974-3-4 (Ebook)

ISBN 978-1-7638974-4-1 (Paperback)

ISBN 978-1-7638974-5-8 (Hardback)

Lord, as I open this book, open my heart.

Quiet the chaos.

Let Your truth sink deep into the places

where fear has made a home.

I'm listening.

I'm willing.

I'm Yours.

TABLE OF CONTENTS

Introduction	1
Week 1: An Anchor For Bad Days	3
Week 2: Honest and True	7
Week 3: The Good Defense	11
Week 4: Beyond the Reality of Anxiety	15
Week 5: Unwrap a New Day	19
Week 6: A Warm Blanket	23
Week 7: Mind Where We Are	27
Week 8: Wired Differently	31
Week 9: Though My Strength Drains Away	35
Week 10: Let the Dawn Break	39
Week 11: To Win Within	43
Week 12: Divine Spa Appointment	47
Week 13: To Not Know and Be Wise	51
Week 14: Love Actually (and Forgive)	55
Week 15: The Fair and The Faithful	59
Week 16: All Within His Control	63
Week 17: Life's Eventuality	67
Week 18: One Step Forward	71
Week 19: Worth Infinitely More	75
Week 20: Glory in the Ordinary	79
Week 21: The Christian Casual	83
Week 22: He Walked in Your Shoes	87
Week 23: The Sweet Choice	91
Week 24: Arresting Love	95

TABLE OF CONTENTS

Week 25: Beyond Fair Weather	99
Week 26: Shared Pilgrimage	103
Week 27: Even in the Tunnel	107
Week 28: My True Portrait	111
Week 29: To Win the War	115
Week 30: He Meets You More Than Halfway	119
Week 31: A New Friend	123
Week 32: Known Fully	127
Week 33: Neither Alone nor Lonely	131
Week 34: The True and Worthy You	135
Week 35: Strong as Paul	139
Week 36: Always According to God's Plan	143
Week 37: Rest for the Mind	147
Week 38: Trying and Transforming	151
Week 39: Common and Communal Peace	155
Week 40: Two-Fold Power	159
Week 41: Travel Light	163
Week 42: Walk Side-by-Side	167
Week 43: The Light in Laughter	171
Week 44: Do Life Together	175
Week 45: In the Cheerleader's Presence	179
Week 46: The Reason to Trust	183
Week 47: Life-Giving Love	187
Week 48: Boasting of the Weak	191
Week 49: Community of Love	195

TABLE OF CONTENTS

Week 50: Tunneling Together — 199

Week 51: Blessed Hopefulness — 203

Week 52: The Healer's Heart — 207

What's Next? — 212

About the Author — 214

Introduction

Anxiety has a way of creeping in, doesn't it? One minute you're fine, and the next your mind is racing, your heart is pounding, and everything feels overwhelming.

My anxiety journey began during a period of relentless entrepreneurial demands. For years, I pushed myself through 14-hour days, seven days a week, to build my business. When it began to struggle, I exhausted myself trying to resurrect it, only to ultimately face failure. During this same intense period, I suffered the devastating loss of my brother, sister, and mother—all within just 18 months of each other.

This perfect storm of professional pressure and personal grief created the conditions for severe burnout and debilitating anxiety.

In our crushing moments of anxiety, our hearts often struggle to grasp that God remains beside us, guiding everything and caring about each tiny detail of our journey. I certainly questioned it when my world collapsed around me. That's why I created this devotional—to help you bridge that gap between what you know in your head and what you feel in your anxious moments.

I want to be clear: faith is powerful, but addressing clinical anxiety often requires multiple approaches. This devotional offers spiritual support that complements—not replaces—other treatments like therapy, medication, or stress-management techniques. If you're struggling with severe anxiety, I encourage you to work with healthcare providers while using this as your spiritual resource.

This devotional is designed to work hand-in-hand with the main *"From Worry to Worship"* book. Anxiety is complex; it affects our bodies, our thoughts, our relationships, and our spiritual lives. These weekly entries are **intentionally focused**—providing spiritual touchstones that you can return to throughout your week rather than exhaustive explorations.

While each book stands alone, together they create a complementary approach to anxiety through faith, combining easy-to-digest weekly guidance with a more thorough exploration in the main book.

Many readers find that using both resources deepens their healing journey and provides the perfect balance of instruction and daily guidance as they move from worry to worship.

In this devotional, each week, you'll tackle a different aspect of anxiety, grounding your approach in Scripture while offering practical ways to apply God's truth to your specific struggles. Over the next 52 weeks, you'll discover how to:

- Swap anxious thoughts with calmness

- Relax in the midst of uncertainty

- Build resilience through biblical truth

- Transform worry into worship, even on difficult days

Each devotional features Scripture addressing anxiety, thoughtful reflections connecting God's Word to your life, reflective questions, prayer support, and an affirmation to carry with you. As you grow in trusting God, you'll experience both breakthroughs and setbacks—that's normal in healing. Whether your anxiety is occasional or constant, you'll find support without judgment, only grace and the reminder that God's peace is available even in your most anxious moments.

So take a deep breath. Turn the page. And let's get you on your path to healing From Worry to Worship, one week at a time.

With love and God bless,

Grace Andrews

P.S. If you find that this devotional touches your heart, it would be a blessing if you could share a brief review on Amazon. Your review will help reach other Christians struggling with anxiety who might not otherwise find this devotional. Thank you for sharing your love and helping in this work!

Week 1: An Anchor For Bad Days

"But you, Lord, are a shield around me, my glory, the One who lifts my head high."

(PSALM 3:3)

There are days when nothing feels right. And maybe, for you, most days feel this way. Yet the wonder that keeps you going is that you make it through. More than that—you see the light of a new day.

When nothing within you feels right, the truth stands firm—the Lord is your shield. He makes a covering around you, protecting and preserving you. Arrows by day and night come charging at you, yet they do not harm you. What a mighty and sweet embrace, holding you every moment you breathe.

And oh, your glory. Imagine that—while you feel swept about by life, you are anchored by this constant. You hold the glory of the Lord within you. There is an unchanging strength and light bestowed upon you. Even a single moment of clarity can propel you through the day, reminding you that the Lord is ever with you. How can you not stand tall amid these days?

A Prayer in Times of Anxiety

Lord, my shield and glory, when anxiety overwhelms me, lift my head high. When I cannot find strength within myself, remind me of Your protection surrounding me. Help me to rest in Your mighty embrace and trust in Your unfailing presence, even when nothing feels right. Amen.

STILLING THE STORM WITHIN

In what specific situations do you most struggle with anxiety, and how might viewing God as your shield change your perspective in those moments?

The devotional speaks of God as "the One who lifts my head high." When anxiety makes you feel defeated, what practical steps can you take to remember God's ability to restore your dignity and confidence?

How has God been your glory in past difficulties, and what does it mean to you personally that you "hold the glory of the Lord within you" during anxious times?

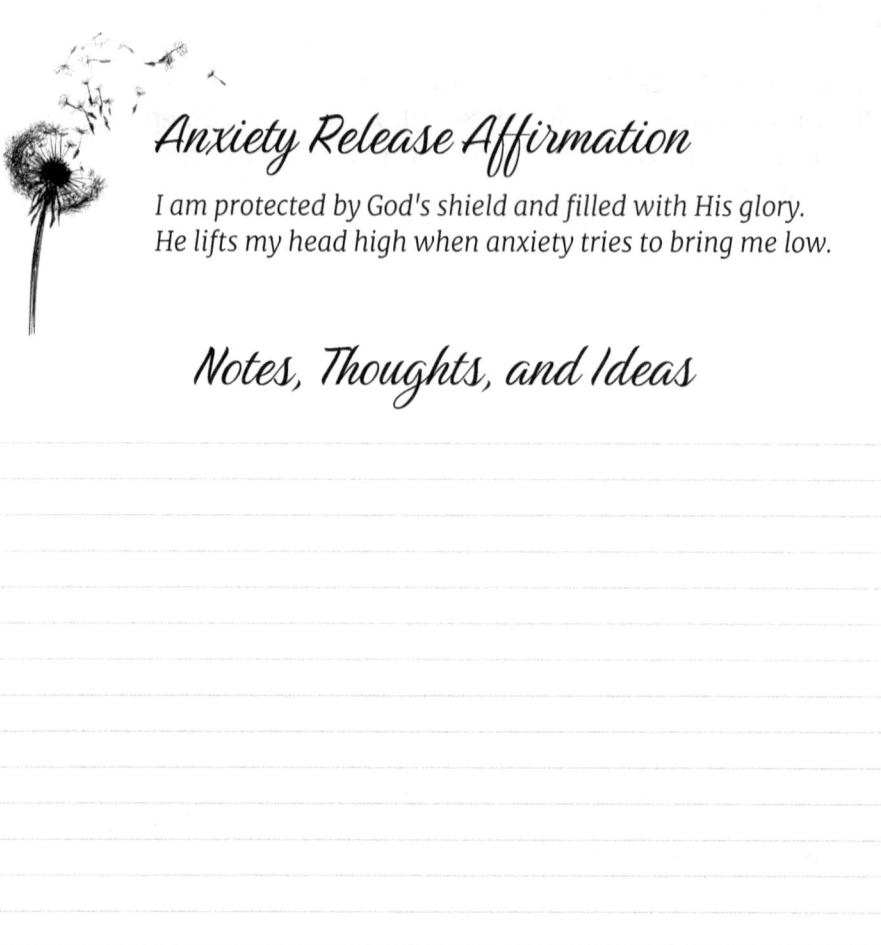

Anxiety Release Affirmation

I am protected by God's shield and filled with His glory.
He lifts my head high when anxiety tries to bring me low.

Notes, Thoughts, and Ideas

ENCOURAGEMENT FOR THE WEEK AHEAD

Remember that anxiety does not define who you are or what you can become. The same God who is your shield has promised never to leave you nor forsake you. When anxious thoughts flood your mind, pause and recall that you have made it through difficult days before—not by your own strength, but because the Lord has been faithfully holding you.

Let each new morning serve as a testament to His ongoing protection and care. Your worth comes not from perfect days or flawless performance, but from being deeply loved by the God who lifts your head high even when you cannot do so yourself.

Week 2: Honest and True

*"How long, Lord? Will you forget me forever?
How long will you hide your face from me?"*

(PSALM 13:1)

After enduring the long wait, you feel your faith grow weary and faint. You never imagined it would take this long or be this trying.

And in your helplessness, you ache all the more, as if God is distant and you are all alone. The One you believed would never abandon you feels absent, as if He is nowhere near.

But just like the psalmist, God welcomes your raw and unfiltered emotions. You can cry out to Him with your hurts and disappointments, even project onto Him all that feels wrong. Because His love for you is mighty, this does not offend Him. He journeys with you still, even in those moments when you blame Him.

And then you realize—because faith remains and because God Himself sustains your faith—that when you have poured your heart out to Him, He is ever with you. His love is unfailing.

When all else fails, He is the One you can always count on.

A Prayer in Times of Anxiety

Heavenly Father, when my heart feels forgotten and my soul weary, hear my honest cry. In these moments when You seem far away, remind me that You receive my raw emotions without judgment. Hold me close when I cannot feel Your presence. Renew my trust as I pour out my heart to You. Thank You that even in my anxious waiting, Your unfailing love remains my constant hope. Amen.

STILLING THE STORM WITHIN

When have you felt like the psalmist, wondering if God has forgotten you in your anxiety? How did you eventually sense His presence again?

The devotional mentions "pouring your heart out to God." What stops you from being completely honest with God about your feelings of abandonment or disappointment?

How might acknowledging your raw emotions to God, rather than hiding them, actually strengthen your faith during times of anxiety and waiting?

Anxiety Release Affirmation

Even when I feel forgotten in my anxiety, God receives my honest cries and holds me in His unfailing love that never abandons me.

Notes, Thoughts, and Ideas

_____
_____
_____
_____
_____
_____
_____
_____
_____
_____
_____
_____

ENCOURAGEMENT FOR THE WEEK AHEAD

The path through anxiety often feels lonely, as if God has turned away. Yet there is holy ground in these honest cries—the very act of calling out "How long, Lord?" affirms that you still believe He listens. Your questions don't push God away; they draw Him near. The psalmist shows us that faith isn't about perfect feelings but perfect honesty.

When you voice your doubts and fears, you join countless believers throughout history who found that after the lament comes renewed trust. Your anxious heart matters to God. He catches every tear, hears every whispered worry, and stays beside you—not despite your questions, but right in the middle of them.

Week 3: The Good Defense

"He has alienated my family from me; my acquaintances are completely estranged from me. ...I am nothing but skin and bones; I have escaped only by the skin of my teeth."

(JOB 19:13, 20)

Have you ever felt like there's no one to call your family? Have friends deserted you? And as if that weren't enough, perhaps your own body reflects your misery. This was Job's lot. And while you may not experience such severe loss, you know what undeniable pain feels like. You struggle, you suffer, and much of it happens in silence.

Then comes that tipping point when, like Job, you can no longer keep silent. His friends accused him of great sin, insisting that he must have done wrong to suffer so much. He spoke in his defense, crying out in agony. Yet, unbeknownst to him, it was Satan who afflicted him, and God had set boundaries to preserve His servant's life.

Even the righteous can blurt out words that accuse God. And yet, He remains by your side, your defender. He patiently leads you to the truth of His goodness and greatness. Oh, how finite your vision is—but when you look to God, you see the majesty of your King and the love of your Father. He can help you through the worst of times.

A Prayer in Times of Anxiety

Father, in those moments when I feel utterly alone, abandoned by friends and family, remind me that You remain constant. When my body and spirit feel wasted away, when I've barely escaped with just the skin of my teeth, draw me close. Help me see beyond my limited vision to Your greater purpose. Like Job, I may not understand Your ways, but I trust Your loving boundaries protect me even in my deepest anguish. Amen.

STILLING THE STORM WITHIN

When have you felt isolated and misunderstood like Job, and how did God reveal His presence during that time?

_____
_____
_____
_____
_____
_____
_____
_____
_____
_____
_____
_____
_____
_____
_____

How do you respond when anxiety causes you to feel physically and emotionally depleted?

In what ways might God be setting protective boundaries around you even in your current struggles?

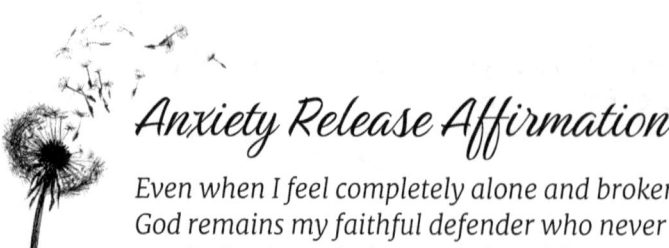

Anxiety Release Affirmation

Even when I feel completely alone and broken down to nothing, God remains my faithful defender who never abandons me and sets loving boundaries around my life to protect me.

Notes, Thoughts, and Ideas

ENCOURAGEMENT FOR THE WEEK AHEAD

When anxiety strips you of relationships and leaves you feeling physically broken, remember that you're in good company with faithful servants like Job. Your suffering isn't punishment—it's a space where God stands as your defender despite what others might say. You may cry out in your pain, even with words that seem to accuse God, but He doesn't abandon you. Instead, He stays close, patiently revealing His goodness when you're ready to see it. Your finite vision can't grasp His infinite plan, but when you look to Him, you'll find the majesty of your King and the tender love of your Father carrying you through your darkest moments.

Week 4: Beyond the Reality of Anxiety

"Do not be anxious about anything, but in every situation, by prayer and petition, with thanksgiving, present your requests to God. And the peace of God, which transcends all understanding, will guard your hearts and your minds in Christ Jesus."

(PHILIPPIANS 4:6-7)

The reality of anxiety is acknowledged in the Bible. God understands how anxiety fragments your heart and clouds your judgment, making wise decisions seem impossible. But another reality is also taught—the reality of peace that surpasses the chaos within and around you.

The practical advice given to you is that even when you are anxious, you can channel your energy into entering the presence of God through prayer and holding onto the peace He grants. You can pray more and pray often. He, whose providence governs all of creation, also attends to your personal needs. It is nothing short of magnificent that the eternal sovereign is also lovingly intimate. He calls you to involve Him in your daily life. The trivial things in your life are not insignificant to God.

Peace is the precious treasure that Satan seeks to steal from you so that you live in misery. But Jesus, who truly loves you, tells you to cherish your peace. Live in the reality of the peace that He gives.

A Prayer in Times of Anxiety

Father, when anxiety overwhelms me, help me remember Your invitation to bring everything to You. Right now, I surrender my worries and fears through prayer, with a heart of thanksgiving despite my circumstances. I choose to trust Your promise of peace that goes beyond my understanding. Guard my heart and mind in Christ Jesus, replacing my anxiety with Your perfect peace that no situation can disturb. Thank You for caring about even the smallest details of my life. Amen.

STILLING THE STORM WITHIN

What specific anxieties am I holding onto that I need to surrender to God through prayer today?

How might practicing gratitude even in difficult situations change my perspective on my current worries?

When have I experienced God's peace that "transcends all understanding," and how can I remember that experience during anxious moments?

Anxiety Release Affirmation

The same God who governs all creation attends lovingly to my personal needs, offering me a peace that surpasses understanding when I bring my anxieties to Him in prayer.

Notes, Thoughts, and Ideas

_____
_____
_____
_____
_____
_____
_____
_____
_____
_____
_____
_____

ENCOURAGEMENT FOR THE WEEK AHEAD

Anxiety is real—God acknowledges this. He sees how it tears at your heart and clouds your judgment. But He offers you something more powerful: His peace. This isn't simplistic advice to "just stop worrying." It's an invitation to channel your anxious energy into prayer, bringing even your trivial concerns to the One who finds nothing about you insignificant.

Your eternal sovereign is also intimately acquainted with your daily struggles. Satan wants to steal your peace and leave you in misery, but Jesus calls you to guard this precious treasure. Live today in the reality that His peace is available even when understanding isn't.

Week 5: Unwrap a New Day

"For the Spirit God gave us does not make us timid but gives us power, love, and self-discipline."

(2 TIMOTHY 1:7)

I'm just too weak. I've always been weak. Giving in and giving up have defined my life.

Have you ever battled against this thought and belief? Before you trusted in Jesus, perhaps you never heard a different message about yourself. And even now, this thought crosses your mind more often than you'd like. But Jesus calms your fears and frees you from the lie!

You have been given something no one can steal from you. With the Holy Spirit, you wield the abundant life promised by Jesus. Being weak is not who you are. With God's divine power, you can overcome and be victorious. With His love, you can serve and give of yourself to others. As He trains you in self-discipline, you can grow more and more in the truth.

This gift, however, can be tucked away in the corner of your mind, left unwrapped. But you can unwrap it today and bring it to the forefront of your mind and life each day. How amazing today can be.
Seize it!

A Prayer in Times of Anxiety

Lord, forgive me for the times I've believed the lie that I am defined by weakness. Thank You for Your Spirit that fills me with power, love, and self-discipline. When anxiety tells me I can't overcome, remind me of the gift You've given—a gift no one can take away. Help me unwrap this treasure daily, bringing it from the corner of my mind to the center of my thoughts. I choose to live in Your strength today, not my weakness. Thank You for making me more than my fears. Amen.

STILLING THE STORM WITHIN

In what areas of your life do you most often hear the whisper "I'm just too weak"?

_____
_____
_____
_____
_____
_____
_____
_____
_____
_____
_____
_____
_____
_____
_____
_____
_____
_____

How might your day look different if you consciously unwrapped God's gift of power, love, and self-discipline each morning?

What specific fear or anxiety could you face today with the power of the Holy Spirit rather than timidity?

Anxiety Release Affirmation

God's Spirit has given me power, love, and self-discipline—not timidity—and I can unwrap this gift daily to overcome my anxieties.

Notes, Thoughts, and Ideas

ENCOURAGEMENT FOR THE WEEK AHEAD

Anxiety wants you to believe weakness is your identity. It's the lie you've heard repeated throughout your life. But God says otherwise. The Spirit He gave you isn't some small token—it's the power that raised Christ from the dead now living in you! This isn't positive thinking; it's divine reality. You have been fundamentally changed.

The gift is already yours, but it awaits your daily decision to unwrap it, to live from this truth rather than from fear. Today can be amazing not because circumstances are perfect, but because God's power in you is greater than anxiety's grip. Seize this day with the confident knowledge that timidity is not your portion!

Week 6: A Warm Blanket

*"Even though I walk through the darkest valley,
I will fear no evil, for you are with me;
your rod and your staff, they comfort me"*

(PSALM 23:4)

What can make a winter day bearable? Staying home, sipping a warm cup of chocolate or coffee, and wrapping yourself in a weighted blanket. But how do you weather the cold of the soul?

David says, *"Even though I walk through the darkest valley..."*
Valleys are a metaphor that contrasts with what mountains represent. Valleys are hedged in, surrounded. While mountains bring blissful moments, valleys bring times of overwhelming sadness.

Some translations say, "through the valley of the shadow of death." Death casts a shadow, freezing your spirit. Imagine the absence of light—immensely frightening. The weight feels unbearable. But you can walk through unharmed because you do not walk alone. You have a sure, warm security blanket.

The Lord's light never departs from you. It wraps around you, keeping you warm through the night. What a comfort!

A Prayer in Times of Anxiety

Shepherd of my soul, when I walk through dark valleys of anxiety and fear, help me feel Your presence wrapping around me like a warm blanket. When death's shadow chills my spirit and mountains of joy seem distant, remind me that You never leave my side. Your rod protects me from danger, and Your staff guides me forward when I can't see the path. Thank You for being my comfort in the coldest moments of my life. I choose to fear no evil because You are with me. Amen.

STILLING THE STORM WITHIN

When have you felt like you were walking through "the darkest valley" in your life, and how did you experience God's presence there?

_____
_____
_____
_____
_____
_____
_____
_____
_____
_____
_____
_____
_____
_____
_____

How does knowing that God is with you like a "sure, warm security blanket" change how you face anxiety today?

What specific "rod and staff" has God provided to comfort and guide you through your current valley?

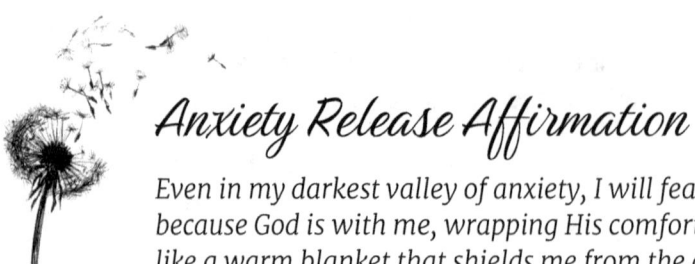

Anxiety Release Affirmation

Even in my darkest valley of anxiety, I will fear no evil because God is with me, wrapping His comfort around me like a warm blanket that shields me from the cold.

Notes, Thoughts, and Ideas

_____
_____
_____
_____
_____
_____
_____
_____
_____
_____
_____

ENCOURAGEMENT FOR THE WEEK AHEAD

We all face valleys—those times when anxiety surrounds us, when we feel hedged in by shadows with no escape. The darkness can freeze your spirit and make each step forward seem impossible. But remember, you never walk these valleys alone. The Good Shepherd walks beside you, His rod defending you from dangers unseen, His staff guiding you when the path disappears. His presence is your warm blanket in the bitter cold of fear. When anxiety wraps its icy fingers around your heart, God's light never departs. It penetrates the darkness, wrapping you in security that no circumstance can tear away. Take the next step through your valley, warmed by the unfailing presence of your Shepherd.

Week 7: Mind Where We Are

"Since, then, you have been raised with Christ, set your hearts on things above, where Christ is, seated at the right hand of God. Set your minds on things above, not on earthly things."

(COLOSSIANS 3:1-2)

How stressful life is today. With the internet and social media, the voices that put you down—both within and without—are amplified. But the Lord's voice is the truth, and it lifts you up.

The Lord tells you in Colossians 3:1-2 that you have been raised with Christ. This is your spiritual reality. You might not feel it, but it is true. You have been made completely new, transported from darkness to light and from bondage to freedom. Your spiritual sphere has changed completely!

In response, you are to set your mind on things above. When you practice mindfulness, you tap into your Christ-ableness to rise above your situation. This is meant to be your constant and persevering mindset until your final breath. It's not occasional; it's not seasonal—it's intentional and continual. You endure to the finish as you set your heart and mind on things above!

A Prayer in Times of Anxiety

Father, when stress overwhelms me and the negative voices grow loud, help me remember that I have been raised with Christ. In moments when anxiety clouds my vision, gently redirect my focus to things above. Remind me of my true identity—transported from darkness to light, from bondage to freedom. When earthly concerns pull my attention downward, lift my gaze to where Christ sits at Your right hand. Thank You for the Christ-ableness that empowers me to rise above my situation. Amen.

STILLING THE STORM WITHIN

What earthly concerns or anxieties currently dominate your thoughts, and how might setting your mind on things above change your perspective on them?

How does remembering your spiritual reality—that you've been raised with Christ—impact how you view your current struggles?

What practical steps can you take today to practice this "Christ-ableness" mindfulness when anxiety tries to overwhelm you?

Anxiety Release Affirmation

I have been raised with Christ and transported from darkness to light, so I can set my mind on things above and rise above anxiety through the power of my new spiritual reality.

Notes, Thoughts, and Ideas

ENCOURAGEMENT FOR THE WEEK AHEAD

The voices of anxiety can be deafening in today's connected world. They whisper constantly that you're not enough, that your situation is hopeless. But remember—your spiritual sphere has completely changed! The truth of who you are isn't found in these voices but in Christ's declaration over you. This mindfulness isn't a temporary fix or occasional practice—it's your new way of living. Each time anxiety rises, intentionally redirect your thoughts upward. This isn't denial of your struggles but recognition of a greater reality. Your spiritual position with Christ gives you the power to persevere through every anxious moment. Keep setting your heart and mind on things above until your very last breath!

Week 8: Wired Differently

"Therefore, there is now no condemnation for those who are in Christ Jesus, because through Christ Jesus the law of the Spirit who gives life has set you free from the law of sin and death."

(ROMANS 8:1)

Immersed in cultures full of guilt and shame, you might struggle with self-doubt, self-pity, and putting yourself down. You've heard these negative messages, and you've believed them. You know this pattern is harmful, but somehow, it's a downhill slope you can't seem to escape. You're wired to be hard on yourself; even when you're exhausted, you use your last bit of strength to sabotage yourself.

But listen now. Listen to the Voice who speaks only the truth and knows the truth of who you are. You are so loved to be chosen to give His life for. The One who sees all your days and moments tells you that you are worthy of love. The evidence is the Cross, through which He set you free for the truly good life.

And keep listening to this. So, when your inner voice makes you feel unworthy, His voice will anchor you. He will rewire you to believe who you are according to the Gospel. It's a long journey, but He can take you there.

A Prayer in Times of Anxiety

Father, I confess that I'm often wired for self-condemnation, caught in cycles of guilt and shame that feel inescapable. Thank You for Your voice of truth that speaks louder than my inner critic. When I slip into self-sabotage and doubt, remind me that the Cross stands as evidence of my worth to You. Thank You that through Christ, there is no condemnation for me—only freedom and life. Help me listen to Your truth today until it rewires how I think about myself. Amen.

STILLING THE STORM WITHIN

How does the reality of "no condemnation" in Christ challenge the guilt and shame messages you've internalized?

When do you most often find yourself sliding down that "downhill slope" of self-deprecation, and how might remembering Romans 8:1 interrupt that pattern?

What specific negative thought patterns do you need God to "rewire" in your mind today?

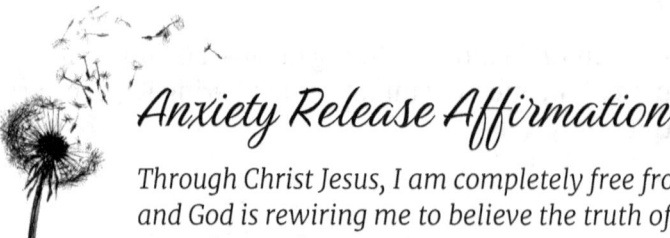

Anxiety Release Affirmation

Through Christ Jesus, I am completely free from condemnation, and God is rewiring me to believe the truth of who I am according to the Gospel.

Notes, Thoughts, and Ideas

_____
_____
_____
_____
_____
_____
_____
_____
_____
_____
_____
_____

ENCOURAGEMENT FOR THE WEEK AHEAD

The voices of guilt and shame have trained you well, haven't they? That downward spiral feels almost automatic—a well-worn path your thoughts travel without effort. But God's truth stands in direct opposition to this wiring. His voice declares what feels impossible to believe: you are worth dying for. The Cross wasn't plan B—it was His determined choice because of His love for you. This rewiring doesn't happen overnight. The journey from self-condemnation to freedom is often slow, with steps forward and back. But each time you choose to listen to His voice over your inner critic, new pathways form. His truth begins to anchor you when anxiety and shame try to pull you under. Keep listening. Keep believing. He will take you there.

Week 9: Though My Strength Drains Away

"Those who hope in the Lord will renew their strength"

(ISAIAH 40:31)

The darkness of despair is crippling. Just when you think you've reached the worst point, you suddenly find yourself falling into an even deeper pit. The darkness sips every ounce of your strength and drains every glimmer of your light. Keeping on feels impossible.

But the Lord's steadfast might catches and carries you through! He can and will renew your strength and supply even greater might to your heart, mind, and body.

When you can't strive anymore, surrender to Him and rest in Him. You can tell Him you just can't anymore, but entrust Him to keep you. Let Him nourish your body with good food and your mind with divine assurance.

Look to Him and hope in Him. Even and especially when all you see is darkness, know that even that darkness bows to the Lord, and He is never away from you.

The Almighty Lord you worship is the One who brings out the good in your impossible.

A Prayer in Times of Anxiety

Lord, when my strength feels drained by anxiety, I turn to You as my source of renewal. Thank You that even in moments of deepest despair, Your steadfast might catches and carries me. I surrender to Your loving care, knowing You nourish my body, mind, and soul with exactly what I need. Fill me with fresh strength and divine assurance as I place my hope in You. Thank You that darkness must bow to Your light, and that You are working good even in what seems impossible to me. Amen.

STILLING THE STORM WITHIN

When have you experienced God renewing your strength after a period of feeling depleted, and what did that renewal look like?

_____
_____
_____
_____
_____
_____
_____
_____
_____
_____
_____
_____
_____
_____

What specific ways can you practice hoping in the Lord today when anxiety challenges your perspective?

How might shifting from striving to surrendering change your experience with anxiety right now?

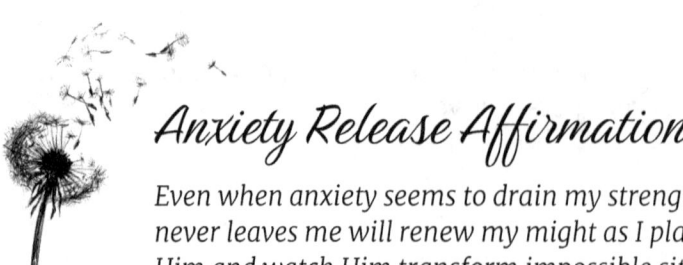

Anxiety Release Affirmation

Even when anxiety seems to drain my strength, the Lord who never leaves me will renew my might as I place my hope in Him and watch Him transform impossible situations.

Notes, Thoughts, and Ideas

ENCOURAGEMENT FOR THE WEEK AHEAD

The darkness of despair may feel overwhelming, but it never has the final word in your story. When anxiety drains your strength and keeping on feels impossible, this becomes your sacred invitation to experience God's renewing power. He stands ready to supply fresh might to your heart, mind, and body. Rather than exhausting yourself with striving, discover the freedom of surrender. Tell Him honestly when you can't go further, then watch as He carries you forward. Let Him nourish you completely—body and soul. As you look to Him and place your hope in His promises, even the darkest moments bow to His light. The Almighty Lord specializes in bringing unexpected good from seemingly impossible situations.

Week 10: Let the Dawn Break

*"Because of the Lord's great love we are not consumed,
for his compassions never fail.
They are new every morning;
great is your faithfulness."*

(LAMENTATIONS 3:22-23)

O to have beautiful days and splendid thoughts. But another reality consumes you. It's an unpleasant season and a disheartening vision. While others live the dream, you struggle through a nightmare.

But the greater reality redeems you. Your Heavenly Father's love and compassion are unfailing. They never run out. Your trials may be many, but His love and compassion are more! On your own, surely you cannot make it. But God is with you and for you.

The night, however long, shall always end, and a new day shall always dawn. For by His faithfulness, He commands them so. Hold on, He is holding you, too. What comes along are divine favors and great outworkings of the Holy Spirit ready to meet you along your day's road.

So, sleep through the night. Let His light ever guide you through. Seize the day as you trust the good Lord to seize your heart.

A Prayer in Times of Anxiety

Faithful Father, when life consumes me with unpleasant seasons and disheartening visions, thank You that Your compassions are new every morning. When I feel trapped in a nightmare while others seem to live the dream, remind me that Your unfailing love is my greater reality. Thank You that the darkest night always gives way to dawn because You command it so. Help me trust that You're holding me through every trial and that Your divine favors await me along today's road. Amen.

STILLING THE STORM WITHIN

When have you felt consumed by difficult circumstances, and how did you experience God's compassions meeting you in that place?

What would it look like to truly believe that God's mercies are "new every morning" in your current season of anxiety?

How might trusting God's faithfulness change how you approach both the night seasons and the dawn of new days in your life?

Anxiety Release Affirmation

Because of God's great love I will not be consumed by anxiety, for His compassions never fail but are made new for me with each morning's dawn.

Notes, Thoughts, and Ideas

_____
_____
_____
_____
_____
_____
_____
_____
_____
_____
_____

ENCOURAGEMENT FOR THE WEEK AHEAD

The contrast can feel so stark—others living their dreams while you trudge through what feels like an endless nightmare. But a greater reality exists beyond what consumes your thoughts today. Your Heavenly Father's love and compassion never run dry, never diminish, and He never flinches at your broken pieces. Your trials may multiply, but His mercies multiply faster! On your own, the anxiety might overwhelm you, but you're never on your own. God stands with you and for you. No night lasts forever—dawn always breaks through the darkness because God has ordained it so. Hold fast to this truth when anxiety threatens to consume you. Divine favors and fresh workings of the Spirit await you on today's path.

Week 11: To Win Within

> *"When anxiety was great within me,
> your consolation brought me joy."*
>
> (PSALM 94:19)

Overthinking hardly captures it. The restless thoughts in your mind weigh heavily on you, creating a sense of being overwhelmed. You try to find relief in sleep, but even then, true rest seems elusive. When you first wake up, that familiar knot of worry returns to your stomach. This persistent anxiety feels like a constant companion that's difficult to shake.

Also within, there is the calm and constant Councilor. He never departs, which in itself is a wonderful consolation. Rather, He ever leads you to the truth. In turn, you experience peace and joy. This is the miracle of faith. While the natural order dictates that you remain in fear, God's embracing presence can pierce through that fog.

If only for a moment you believe, His abiding presence fills you, yes, even to overflowing. When you choose to get up and face what you would rather escape, the cloud of witnesses are honored, and they cheer you. The ones who know your suffering become encouraged by you. And what a privilege, the Lord is glorified by you!

A Prayer in Times of Anxiety

Lord, when my mind races with anxiety and restless thoughts weigh me down, remind me of Your constant presence. Even when sleep doesn't bring rest and worry greets me each morning, Your consolation can still break through. Thank You that You never depart from me. When I'm tempted to stay trapped in fear, help me believe—even for a moment—that Your peace can pierce through the fog of my anxiety. Fill me with Your presence until joy overflows, giving me courage to face what I'd rather escape. Amen.

STILLING THE STORM WITHIN

When anxiety feels overwhelming, what specific consolations from God have brought you moments of joy in the past?

How does knowing that the Holy Spirit is your "calm and constant Councilor" change how you view your anxious thoughts?

What situation are you currently trying to escape that God might be calling you to face with His strengthening presence?

Anxiety Release Affirmation

Even when anxiety feels great within me, God's constant presence and consolation can pierce through the fog of fear and fill me with unexpected joy.

Notes, Thoughts, and Ideas

ENCOURAGEMENT FOR THE WEEK AHEAD

The battle against anxiety often feels like an internal war you can't win. Those racing thoughts seem to have the upper hand, robbing you of rest and peace. But remember—also within you dwells the calm and constant Councilor who never leaves your side. This is your miracle of faith: when natural circumstances dictate fear, God's embracing presence offers an alternative reality. It takes just a moment of belief for His presence to begin filling the spaces anxiety has claimed. When you find the courage to rise and face what anxiety tells you to avoid, heaven notices. The cloud of witnesses cheers you on, others walking similar paths find hope in your steps, and the Lord Himself is glorified by your faith-filled movement forward.

Week 12: Divine Spa Appointment

"Come to me, all who are weary and burdened, and I will give you rest."

(MATTHEW 11:28)

You are not immune to exhaustion and weariness of heart. You are human, and you will feel exhausted and exasperated. You suffer from toiling because of the heavy burden placed upon you.

Jesus is calling you. He calls all who are toiling and are being burdened or soul-oppressed. Jesus comes to you and speaks in a language you can understand, for your greatest need is to be restored to God.

Jesus invites us into His heart, to come to Him, for He is the way to know God's truth and peace. Because this is not home, we will be hurt again and again, but there is comfort and divine peace with Him.

When we come to His embrace, even when we don't fully know how life will unfold, life begins to be peaceful, make sense again, and even be seen as wonderful again.

He knows you're struggling on your own. Call out to Him for rescue. Come to Him for His rest.

A Prayer in Times of Anxiety

Lord Jesus, I accept Your invitation to come to You with my weariness and heavy burdens. Like stepping into a healing sanctuary, I enter Your presence to find true rest for my soul. Thank You for understanding my exhaustion and speaking to me in ways I can understand. When life's demands leave me depleted, remind me that Your divine spa of grace is always open, offering restoration no earthly comfort can provide. Refresh me today as I surrender my burdens to You and receive Your perfect peace. Amen.

STILLING THE STORM WITHIN

What specific burdens are making you feel weary right now, and how might bringing them to Jesus change your experience of them?

How is Jesus' invitation to rest different from the world's solutions to exhaustion and anxiety?

When have you experienced the "divine spa" of Christ's presence restoring your peace, and how can you make time for such restoration today?

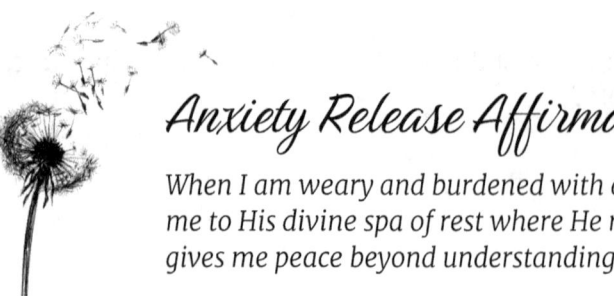

Anxiety Release Affirmation

When I am weary and burdened with anxiety, Jesus invites me to His divine spa of rest where He restores my soul and gives me peace beyond understanding.

Notes, Thoughts, and Ideas

_____
_____
_____
_____
_____
_____
_____
_____
_____
_____
_____
_____

ENCOURAGEMENT FOR THE WEEK AHEAD

Life's demands can leave you spiritually and emotionally depleted, in desperate need of restoration. Like an exclusive spa designed for soul-renewal, Jesus extends His personal invitation to you. This isn't a quick fix or temporary relief—it's a complete restoration that addresses your deepest needs. When you accept His invitation to come, you enter a sacred space where burdens are lifted and weariness dissolves in His presence. The world will continue to bring challenges that exhaust you, but this divine spa remains open, offering continuous renewal. His embrace provides the ultimate spiritual treatment—making life peaceful, meaningful, and wonderful again. No appointment needed. Just come as you are, weary and burdened, and receive the rest only He can give.

Week 13: To Not Know and Be Wise

"If any of you lacks wisdom, you should ask God, who gives generously to all without finding fault, and it will be given to you."

(JAMES 1:5)

You sit where you are, and you don't know what to do. You try to think of a solution, but nothing at all comes to mind. You've come to your wit's end.

To know that you don't know is not being stupid. To know that you don't know and refuse to come to the All-knowing is something else. But you have to know that He is also all-loving and would not shame you for not knowing.

So come to the Father and ask for wisdom. When you come to Him, He is able to remove the veil that keeps you from seeing how things really are.

More than that, He can give you the faith to look into the spiritual realm and how this can turn for your good and His glory. Most importantly, He will give you the grace to do what is wise, that is, obey His will.

A Prayer in Times of Anxiety

Father, in this moment when I sit not knowing what to do, I come to You acknowledging my limited wisdom. Thank You that You don't shame me for not having all the answers. With anxiety clouding my mind and thoughts going nowhere, I ask for Your divine wisdom that sees beyond my circumstances. Remove the veil that keeps me from seeing clearly. Give me faith to trust Your perspective and grace to follow Your guidance. Thank You for giving generously when I simply ask. Amen.

STILLING THE STORM WITHIN

When have you reached your "wit's end" with anxiety, and how did acknowledging your need for God's wisdom help in that situation?

What veils might be keeping you from seeing your current situation clearly, and how might God's wisdom provide a different perspective?

How does knowing that God gives wisdom "without finding fault" change how you approach Him when you're feeling anxious or uncertain?

Anxiety Release Affirmation

When anxiety leaves me not knowing what to do, God gives wisdom generously without shaming me,
and shows me how my situation can work for good.

Notes, Thoughts, and Ideas

ENCOURAGEMENT FOR THE WEEK AHEAD

There's a strange freedom in admitting you don't know what to do. It's not stupidity—it's honesty. The pressure to have all the answers only intensifies anxiety, creating a fog that makes clear thinking impossible. But the God who knows everything invites you to bring your confusion to Him. He won't shame you for your limitations or find fault with your questions. Instead, He offers to lift the veil that anxiety has placed over your perspective. His wisdom reaches beyond your immediate circumstances to reveal spiritual realities you can't see on your own. And most precious of all, He gives you not just insight but the grace to act on it. When anxiety has you paralyzed, remember—wisdom is just a prayer away.

Week 14: Love Actually (and Forgive)

*"Be kind and compassionate to one another,
forgiving each other, just as God forgave you in Christ."*

(EPHESIANS 4:32)

You may think and believe you are a committed believer until you are called to love in actual relationships that involve different personalities, different preferences, different points of view, different backgrounds and values, different upbringings, and different ideals. The reality is that life would be so much easier without relationships. Relationships can be a joy but also burdensome and demanding of commitment.

You have to be patient with others, accepting their brokenness, forgiving them of their offenses, and trusting the Gospel of Christ to bring them to maturity. But can you? If you believe that Christ can love you so much to forgive you, then believe, too, that the heart of the One who forgave you is that same heart that beats in your chest.

Love is a conscious way of life lived for the sake of the other. You are called to love one another, with forgiving as Christ did being an essential aspect. What a difficult command. But whatever He calls you to do, His grace will enable you.

A Prayer in Times of Anxiety

Father, when relationships test my ability to love as You love, remind me of the forgiveness I've received in Christ. When I encounter different personalities, preferences, and perspectives that challenge me, help me extend the same grace You've shown me. In moments when anxiety rises because of relational tensions, soften my heart to respond with kindness and compassion. Thank You that the same heart that forgave me now beats in my chest, empowering me to forgive others. Give me Your strength to love actually—not just in theory. Amen.

STILLING THE STORM WITHIN

How has anxiety affected your ability to forgive others, and how might remembering Christ's forgiveness of you change that response?

Which relationship in your life currently feels most burdensome, and what would it look like to approach it with Christ-like compassion?

When have you experienced the grace of God enabling you to love someone who was difficult to love, and what did that teach you?

Anxiety Release Affirmation

The same heart of Christ that forgave me now beats in my chest, giving me power to be kind, compassionate, and forgiving even in my most challenging relationships.

Notes, Thoughts, and Ideas

ENCOURAGEMENT FOR THE WEEK AHEAD

Relationships reveal the true depth of our faith and the real extent of our anxiety. It's one thing to love in concept, quite another to love actual people with all their complications and imperfections. The tension of different personalities, preferences, and perspectives can trigger deep anxiety that makes us want to withdraw rather than engage. Yet this is precisely where Christ calls us to demonstrate His love most powerfully. Remember—the One who forgave your every fault now lives in you, making possible what seems impossible. Each act of forgiveness is an echo of the grace you've received. Each moment of patience with someone's brokenness reflects God's patience with you. His grace doesn't just save you; it enables you to extend that same grace to others.

Week 15: The Fair and The Faithful

"Do not take revenge...but leave room for God's wrath."

(ROMANS 12:19)

Life is unfair. Only whoever has not lived long enough will disagree with this because they have not been hurt deeply. But God is fair and upright in all His dealings.

You cannot take matters into your hands. You are commanded not to take revenge, primarily to keep you dependent on the Gospel and its power to transform you. God is also protecting you from the evil that may breed from bitterness.

In God's perfect time, all evil shall be defeated. He will demand all to give an account of how they lived. But not yet. Sin will continue to fester. Corruption will worsen. Evil will win many battles, but all within God's bounds. And in His time, the good will show forth its true and eternal power. And good shall reign without end. He calls you to trust Him and His timing.

Painful attacks will come to you, and you will have the choice. Will you overflow with the stench of bitterness and disbelief? Or will you produce a sweet aroma for God?

A Prayer in Times of Anxiety

Lord of justice, when life's unfairness wounds me deeply and anxiety tempts me toward bitterness, help me leave room for Your perfect timing. When revenge feels like my only option for relief, remind me that You see every hurt and will bring all things to account. In moments when evil seems to triumph and my heart races with indignation, steady me with the knowledge that You are both fair and faithful. Thank You for protecting me from the poison of bitterness. Give me strength to choose the sweet aroma of trust over the stench of revenge. Amen.

STILLING THE STORM WITHIN

How has the unfairness of life triggered anxiety in your heart, and what would it look like to truly "leave room for God's wrath" in those situations?

When have you seen bitterness damage someone's life, and how does that observation help you choose a different path?

Which painful attack in your life is currently testing your faith in God's fairness and timing, and how might surrendering it change your experience?

Anxiety Release Affirmation

Even when life seems deeply unfair and anxiety tempts me toward bitterness, I can trust God's perfect justice and timing as I leave room for Him to make all things right.

Notes, Thoughts, and Ideas

ENCOURAGEMENT FOR THE WEEK AHEAD

The deep wounds of injustice can trigger some of our most profound anxiety. When others hurt us and seem to escape consequences, our hearts race with indignation and our minds flood with thoughts of setting things right ourselves. Yet God's command to resist revenge isn't about letting evil win—it's about protecting your soul from bitterness while trusting in perfect justice. Sin will continue its destructive work for now. Evil may claim temporary victories. But all this happens within God's boundaries and timeline. Your choice in painful moments shapes not just your immediate future but your eternal character. The sweet aroma of trust rises above the chaos of injustice, testifying that even in a deeply unfair world, you believe in the One who is perfectly fair.

Week 16: All Within His Control

*"Peace I leave with you; my peace I give you.
I do not give to you as the world gives.
Do not let your hearts be troubled and do not be afraid."*

(JOHN 14:27)

Much in life is beyond your control. Jesus knows this. He knows, too, that you will suffer from being troubled and afraid. So He promises His peace.

The agonies you go through are never futile or in vain. There are moments when you see the wisdom and goodness of God's ways through tragedies in your life. But you also have to be at peace with times when you just cannot make sense of suffering. In heaven, all shall make beautiful sense. But also, maybe you wouldn't need the answers you think you need now. The peace of God is enough.

In the final analysis, you are in Christ; therefore, you are victorious throughout life. Beyond your feelings, this is the truth about you, a constant victor in the light of Jesus' finished work on the Cross. This victorious disposition gives you peace amidst sufferings in this life. So, let go of the desire for control. Delight in God's peace instead.

A Prayer in Times of Anxiety

Lord Jesus, when anxiety tries to steal my peace, remind me of Your words: "Peace I leave with you." When I can't make sense of my suffering, help me trust that You're working even when I can't see it. Thank You for the peace that transcends understanding. Help me to let go of my need for control and rest in Your perfect peace today. Amen.

STILLING THE STORM WITHIN

How am I trying to control situations in my life instead of trusting God's peace?

When I face suffering that doesn't make sense, how do I typically respond and why?

What would it look like for me to live as a "constant victor" despite my feelings of anxiety?

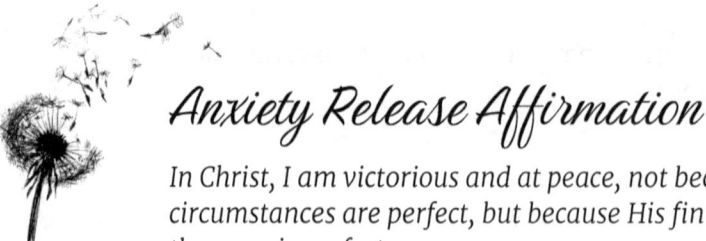

Anxiety Release Affirmation

In Christ, I am victorious and at peace, not because my circumstances are perfect, but because His finished work on the cross is perfect.

Notes, Thoughts, and Ideas

_____
_____
_____
_____
_____
_____
_____
_____
_____
_____
_____
_____

ENCOURAGEMENT FOR THE WEEK AHEAD

When anxiety threatens to overwhelm you, remember that Jesus didn't promise an easy life—He promised His peace in the midst of trouble. This peace isn't dependent on your circumstances making sense. Sometimes the greatest act of faith is to be at peace with not having all the answers right now.

Your victory isn't determined by how you feel but by who holds you. Let go of the illusion of control that feeds your anxiety. Instead, choose to rest in the unshakable truth that in Christ, you are already victorious. This truth remains constant, even when your feelings fluctuate.

Week 17: Life's Eventuality

"Trust in the Lord with all your heart and lean not on your own understanding; in all your ways submit to him, and he will make your paths straight."

(PROVERBS 3:5-6)

In your mind, everything in your life appears temporarily shaken. You see challenges through a lens that magnifies their permanence, convinced of an inevitable outcome that reflects your perspective rather than a changeable reality.

That is true, if the Lord were not in covenant with you. He has seen all that has happened to you and why you now look at life through your perspective. He fully knows what clouds your understanding. Many, if not all people, have some misconception of life, the world, and God because of unfortunate events that afflicted them to their core. Such clearly points to the necessity of humanity for the Lord, who alone sees the grand picture, the true eventuality from the messy present.

However, you have not seen Him and all He has done to preserve you, even with the undeniable evidence of the Cross. So lean on Him. Even when you see all spiraling down, He will catch you and lift you. Remember that on the third day, Jesus rose again. The eventuality is you will rejoice over his mighty goodness.

A Prayer in Times of Anxiety

Heavenly Father, when my mind sees only what's shaken and broken, remind me that You see the complete picture. When I'm convinced things can never change, help me remember Your covenant with me. Thank You for understanding why I see life as I do. Even when I feel everything spiraling down, help me trust that You will catch and lift me, just as You raised Jesus on the third day. Amen.

STILLING THE STORM WITHIN

How have past experiences shaped the lens through which I view my current challenges?

In what ways am I assuming my perspective is the full reality rather than trusting God's broader view?

What would it mean for me to truly believe that rejoicing is my eventual outcome, even when I can't see how?

Anxiety Release Affirmation

God's covenant promises prevail over my temporary perspective. He will lift me up.

Notes, Thoughts, and Ideas

ENCOURAGEMENT FOR THE WEEK AHEAD

Your current perspective isn't the final truth—it's merely how things appear right now through the lens of your experiences. God understands exactly why you see life as you do, and He doesn't condemn you for it. When anxiety convinces you that what you see is all there is, remember that your limited view doesn't change His unlimited power. The same God who raised Jesus on the third day is working behind the scenes in your life too. Your eventual outcome isn't determined by today's challenges but by His faithful covenant with you. Trust that beyond today's spiraling feelings lies the joy of witnessing His mighty goodness in your life.

Week 18: One Step Forward

"Let us draw near to God with a sincere heart and with the full assurance that faith brings, having our hearts sprinkled to cleanse us from a guilty conscience and having our bodies washed with pure water."

(HEBREWS 10:22)

The godly feel guilty, too. And this does not give you the ticket for a pity party. Instead, this assures you that you are not alone in the habit of punishing yourself for giving in to your sinful pattern.

The guilt that keeps you away from the Lord is not by the Holy Spirit. What He gives is the faith to draw near, even when you have acted like the prodigal son. He shakes you up so you can clearly see that you need Him in every moment. And dear child, He sees your sincere heart.

The Lord draws you near to Him and assures you. He does not expect you to do life perfectly, but He does expect that you would hold to Him to love you perfectly. He does not expect wholehearted obedience to be without faltering, but He does expect you to trust Him to love you without failing. Two steps back, but by His grace, three steps forward. Draw Him nearer and nearer.

A Prayer in Times of Anxiety

Father, when I'm trapped in guilt and self-punishment, thank You for reminding me I'm not alone in this struggle. When I feel like running away because of my failures, help me remember that Your Spirit calls me to draw near instead. Thank You for seeing my sincere heart beyond my imperfect actions. Give me the courage to trust Your perfect love, especially when I feel most undeserving of it. Amen.

STILLING THE STORM WITHIN

How has guilt been keeping me away from God rather than drawing me closer to Him?

_____
_____
_____
_____
_____
_____
_____
_____
_____
_____
_____
_____
_____
_____
_____
_____
_____
_____
_____

In what ways am I expecting perfection from myself that God doesn't expect from me?

What would it look like to truly trust God's perfect love even after taking "two steps back"?

Anxiety Release Affirmation

God calls me to draw near in my guilt, not run away, for His perfect love is greater than my imperfect obedience.

Notes, Thoughts, and Ideas

ENCOURAGEMENT FOR THE WEEK AHEAD

When guilt weighs you down, remember it's not meant to keep you trapped in a cycle of self-punishment. The Holy Spirit's conviction always leads you back to God, never away from Him. Your failures don't surprise Him or change His love for you. He sees your sincere heart beneath your struggles.

The path forward isn't perfect obedience—it's perfect trust in His unfailing love. When you take two steps back, His grace enables three steps forward. Don't let guilt build walls between you and God. Instead, let it become the very reason you draw nearer to the One who loves you completely, failures and all.

Week 19: Worth Infinitely More

"Therefore, do not worry about tomorrow, for tomorrow will worry about itself. Each day has enough trouble of its own."

(MATTHEW 6:34)

On an average day, how many dreadful scenarios do you imagine? How many actually happen?

Statistically, what you worry about is improbable. While too tired, worry gets your last ounce of strength. This will absolutely wear you out.

Jesus has you covered. He values you infinitely more than the sparrows and the grass of the field, who thrive on His goodness. And He tells you not to worry, primarily because He is committed to you.

Now He reasons with you. He says worry neither deducts from your problems nor adds to your need for time. Furthermore, Jesus makes it plain that worrying is the habit of the unbeliever. And He knows you can overcome worrying by seeking Him and His promises instead.

Set your concerns aside and let Him hold them for you. When you feel like you only have a bit of strength left, worship Him instead.

A Prayer in Times of Anxiety

Heavenly Father, forgive me for wasting precious energy imagining dreadful scenarios that rarely happen. When worry tries to claim my last bit of strength, help me remember that You have me covered. Thank You for valuing me infinitely more than the sparrows and grass that thrive on Your goodness. Help me set my concerns aside and place them in Your capable hands. When I feel depleted, give me the wisdom to worship rather than worry. Amen.

STILLING THE STORM WITHIN

How much of my mental and emotional energy is spent imagining scenarios that never actually happen and why?

In what ways has worry become my default response instead of seeking God's kingdom first?

What would it look like to truly hand over my concerns to God and use my remaining strength for worship instead?

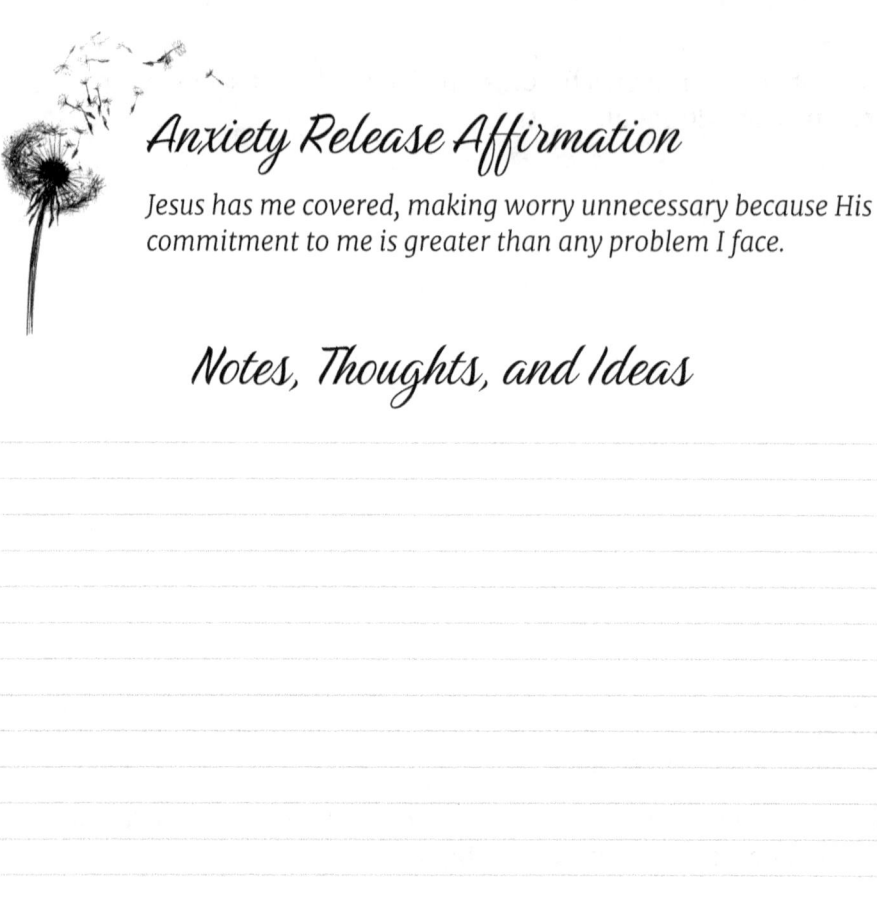

Anxiety Release Affirmation

Jesus has me covered, making worry unnecessary because His commitment to me is greater than any problem I face.

Notes, Thoughts, and Ideas

_____
_____
_____
_____
_____
_____
_____
_____
_____
_____
_____
_____

ENCOURAGEMENT FOR THE WEEK AHEAD

Worry is a thief that steals your energy without solving a single problem. Notice how many of your feared scenarios never materialize, yet claim so much of your strength. This is not how God designed you to live. When Jesus tells you not to worry, it's not a casual suggestion—it's a loving command from Someone who knows exactly what you need. His commitment to you is unwavering. The next time anxiety begins to drain your last reserves, make a deliberate choice to redirect that energy toward worship. This simple act of faith declares that you trust God's provision more than your problems. Your peace isn't found in problem-solving but in person-seeking—seeking Him above all else.

Week 20: Glory in the Ordinary

*"So whether you eat or drink or whatever you do,
do it all for the glory of God."*

(1 CORINTHIANS 10:31)

Martyrs lay down their lives for Jesus. The persecuted love their enemies and win them to the faith. Meanwhile, you find yourself facing the quieter battle of simply beginning each day. You feel like you can't give glory to the Lord.

You rush through your meal and cup of coffee, thinking nothing holy and significant comes from there. You also hurry through washing your dishes and laundry, believing it does not advance His Kingdom. You race through your days, unaware that they are filled with divine appointments to glorify the Lord.

Being mindful that the Lord is present in every moment changes how you live through the uneventful days. You can take great delight from your simple meal and cup of coffee as you thank God for His blessing.

You can do your dishes and laundry while purposefully praying for the advance of His Kingdom. You can be watchful of your days that afford you to seek His will and goodness for you and the world.

A Prayer in Times of Anxiety

Lord, forgive me for believing that my ordinary days lack significance in Your kingdom. When I compare myself to martyrs and the persecuted, I forget that You call me to faithfulness in the quiet moments too. Help me recognize Your presence in my meals, my chores, and my everyday routines. Open my eyes to see the divine appointments hidden within my seemingly uneventful days. Teach me to live mindfully, knowing You are with me in each moment. Amen.

STILLING THE STORM WITHIN

How have I been rushing through ordinary moments without recognizing their spiritual significance?

In what ways might God be inviting me to find His presence in my daily routines?

What would change if I approached each "uneventful" task as a divine appointment with God?

Anxiety Release Affirmation

Every moment of my ordinary day is sacred ground where I can glorify God and advance His kingdom.

Notes, Thoughts, and Ideas

ENCOURAGEMENT FOR THE WEEK AHEAD

The battle to begin each day with anxiety weighing on your heart is no less significant than more visible acts of faith. God doesn't measure devotion by dramatic gestures but by faithful presence in ordinary moments. Your cup of coffee can become a prayer of thanksgiving. Your laundry can be folded as an act of worship. Your seemingly insignificant routines are actually filled with opportunities to experience God's presence.

When anxiety makes you feel disconnected from God's grand purposes, slow down and look more closely at what's right in front of you. His kingdom advances through both martyrs' sacrifices and your mindful presence in everyday moments.

Week 21: The Christian Casual

"Therefore, as God's chosen people, holy and dearly loved, clothe yourselves with compassion, kindness, humility, gentleness, and patience."

(COLOSSIANS 3:12)

If anyone at all understands how essential and critical empathy is, it's you. You know from experience that the walls you've built around yourself have back stories. You wish others knew that you strive with all your might to overcome the crippling thoughts in your mind. Instead of seeking to understand each other's stories, people pass judgment too readily.

So, specifically for you, you understand the wisdom and beauty behind God's command for you to clothe yourself with compassion, kindness, humility, gentleness, and patience. You are called to be full of love because these are its tangible demonstrations. While God is invisible, when you actively wear this wardrobe as your Christian casual attire, people around you have regular reminders of His presence and reality.

How desperately the world needs these qualities. And how rare it is even for many believers to consciously live by this calling. Plant the compassion, kindness, humility, gentleness, and patience you yourself need, because someone like you needs them desperately.

A Prayer in Times of Anxiety

Lord, You know the walls I've built have stories behind them. When others judge without understanding, it hurts deeply. Thank You for showing me the power of empathy through my own struggles. Help me clothe myself with compassion, kindness, humility, gentleness, and patience—especially when my anxiety makes it difficult. Use me to offer others the very understanding I've longed for. May the love You've shown me flow through me to those who need it most. Amen.

STILLING THE STORM WITHIN

How might my personal struggles with anxiety actually equip me to show deeper compassion to others?

Where in my life am I judging others without knowing their back stories?

How can I intentionally "plant" the compassion, kindness, and patience that I myself need?

Anxiety Release Affirmation

My struggles with anxiety uniquely equip me to reflect God's compassion to a world desperate for understanding.

Notes, Thoughts, and Ideas

_____
_____
_____
_____
_____
_____
_____
_____
_____
_____
_____

ENCOURAGEMENT FOR THE WEEK AHEAD

Your anxiety doesn't disqualify you from showing God's love—it may actually deepen your capacity for it. You know firsthand how walls are built brick by brick, each one with its own story. This gives you a rare gift: the ability to look past others' defenses and see the person struggling behind them. When you choose compassion over judgment and kindness over criticism, you're not just following commands—you're making God visible in a world that desperately needs Him. Your small acts of understanding might be exactly what someone else needs to feel less alone in their battle. The empathy you show others today may be the very gift that helps someone else breathe a little easier in their own battle with anxiety.

Week 22: He Walked in Your Shoes

"For we do not have a high priest who is unable to empathize with our weaknesses, but we have one who has been tempted in every way, just as we are—yet he did not sin."

(HEBREWS 4:15)

When you're overwhelmed or misunderstood, it is a blessing to have a few trusted friends you can confide in without fear of judgment. With them, you also wouldn't need to mince your words and consciously filter. You can just be raw and pour out your soul and be completely sure you would be loved no less. You actually are blessed to have Jesus as your friend because He is that and much more!

Jesus understands your struggles because He experienced them Himself. He isn't a distant figure but a Savior who walked through the trials, joys, and pains of human life. He faced temptation, sorrow, fatigue, and even rejection, just like you do.

He doesn't just sympathize from afar; He truly understands the weight of your burdens. Having experienced all the challenges of human life Himself, Jesus invites you to come boldly to Him for help and healing. His compassion for you is deep because He knows exactly what it's like to walk in your shoes. Rest in His empathy today.

A Prayer in Times of Anxiety

Jesus, my truest friend, thank You for being the one I can come to completely unfiltered. When I'm overwhelmed and misunderstood, help me remember I can pour out my raw emotions to You without fear of judgment. Thank You for experiencing human life—with all its trials, sorrows, and pains—so You could truly understand my struggles. When anxiety weighs me down, remind me that You know exactly how it feels. Help me rest in the comfort of Your perfect empathy today. Amen.

STILLING THE STORM WITHIN

How often do I come to Jesus with my unfiltered thoughts and feelings versus trying to "clean them up" first?

In what specific struggles am I forgetting that Jesus has personally experienced human pain and understands me?

What would change in my approach to anxiety if I truly believed Jesus knows exactly what it's like to walk in my shoes?

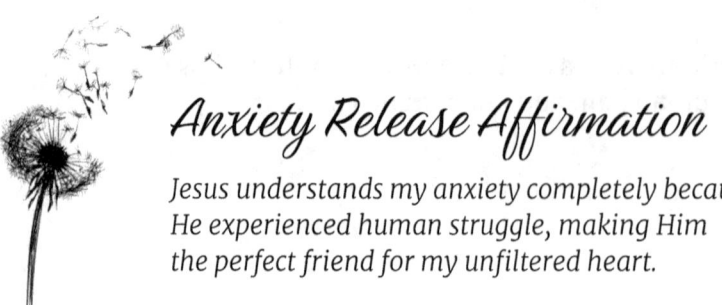

Anxiety Release Affirmation

Jesus understands my anxiety completely because He experienced human struggle, making Him the perfect friend for my unfiltered heart.

Notes, Thoughts, and Ideas

ENCOURAGEMENT FOR THE WEEK AHEAD

When anxiety makes you feel isolated, remember that Jesus offers a friendship unlike any other. He doesn't require you to present a polished version of yourself—He invites your messiest thoughts and rawest emotions. His understanding isn't theoretical; it's experiential. He felt weariness in His body, sorrow in His heart, and the sting of rejection. This is why His invitation to come to Him isn't empty sentiment but a genuine offer from someone who truly gets it. The next time anxiety overwhelms you, imagine sitting with a friend who knows exactly how you feel without you having to explain a thing. That's Jesus, waiting for you with open arms.

Week 23: The Sweet Choice

"Not as I will, but as you will."

(MATTHEW 26:39)

When you're in the middle of an incredibly difficult period of life, you can't point to where you hurt, as somehow your whole being is in agony.

In moments like these, it can feel as if the weight of the world is on your shoulders. You wish to cry, but you also just feel numb within. You also feel as if you're trapped without a choice.

Jesus, in His own moment of anguish, prayed to God, "My Father, if it is possible, let this cup pass from Me; yet not as I will, but as You will."

Even Jesus, in His deepest sorrow, found solace in surrendering to God's will. Isn't He a perfect Lord, who has gone before us that we may follow in His steps?

Surrender may sound like a step for the weak. But in truth, it is a sweet solution to your anguish and a strong statement to imitating Jesus.

Choose surrender.

A Prayer in Times of Anxiety

Father, in this season where my whole being aches with pain, I come to You feeling trapped and numb. When I can't even point to where it hurts because everything hurts, help me remember Jesus in Gethsemane. Like Him, I pray, "If possible, let this cup pass from me; yet not as I will, but as You will." Thank You for a Savior who understands the deepest anguish. Give me the courage to surrender my anxiety to You, knowing that in letting go, I find Your peace. Amen.

STILLING THE STORM WITHIN

In what areas of my anxiety am I still trying to maintain control rather than surrendering to God?

How might my perspective shift if I viewed surrender not as weakness but as following in Jesus' footsteps?

What is one specific burden I need to surrender to God today that feels too heavy for me to carry?

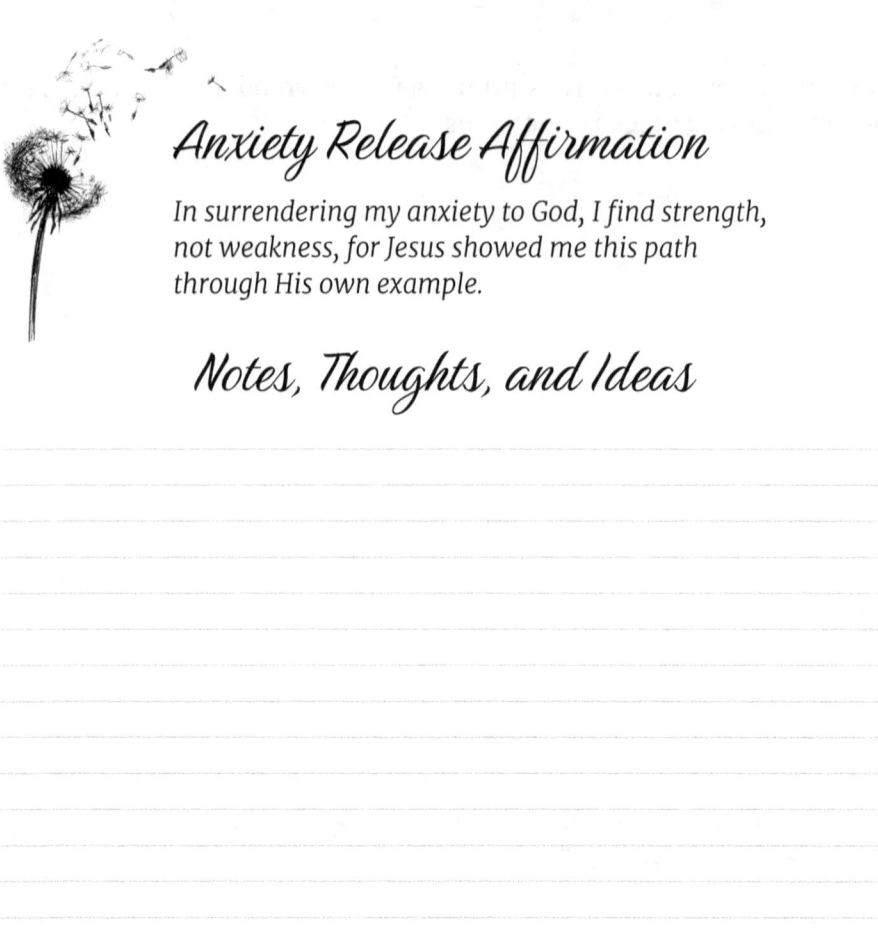

Anxiety Release Affirmation

In surrendering my anxiety to God, I find strength, not weakness, for Jesus showed me this path through His own example.

Notes, Thoughts, and Ideas

ENCOURAGEMENT FOR THE WEEK AHEAD

When anxiety engulfs your entire being and numbness replaces tears, remember you're walking a path Jesus Himself traveled. He knows what it means to wish for another way while accepting what is. Surrender isn't about giving up—it's about acknowledging that some burdens were never meant for your shoulders alone. This letting go is actually a profound act of faith, a declaration that God's wisdom exceeds your understanding. Each time you release your white-knuckled grip on control, you're not displaying weakness but demonstrating the same strength Jesus showed in Gethsemane. The peace waiting on the other side of surrender is His gift to you.

Week 24: Arresting Love

"A new command I give you: Love one another. As I have loved you, so you must love one another. By this everyone will know that you are my disciples, if you love one another."

(JOHN 13:34-35)

How tragic to live in a world where hurt people hurt others. The innocent are attacked, and they also breed hurt. You yourself started without pain and wounds, but can you do anything to arrest this horrid cycle?

You are called to shine God's love with acts of kindness. Kindness is the light of love that restores the faith of the struggling in a world that often feels harsh. By this, you show the world to Whom you truly belong. When you show kindness, you are showing the heart of Jesus to a world in desperate need of it.

Love one another makes plain that you simply have to begin with one step. Don't think too much about the next steps. The next faithful step will become clear. The next person in need of love will be right before you. May His love flow through you, making the world a little warmer, one act at a time.

A Prayer in Times of Anxiety

Father, in a world where hurt cycles endlessly, use me to break this pattern. When I'm tempted to pass my pain to others, remind me of Your calling to shine with kindness instead. Thank You for showing me the way through Jesus. Give me courage to take that first step of love, even when I can't see the full path ahead. Help me to be Your hands and heart to the hurting people You place in my path today. May Your love flow through me, bringing warmth to this cold world. Amen.

STILLING THE STORM WITHIN

How have I been passing on my own hurts to others rather than breaking the cycle with kindness?

What is one small act of kindness I could do today that might restore someone's faith in goodness?

Who is the "next person in need of love" right before me that I might be overlooking?

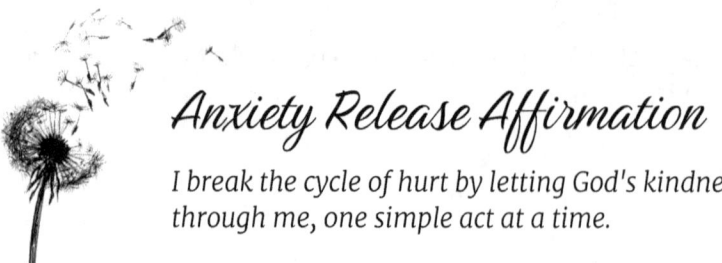

Anxiety Release Affirmation

I break the cycle of hurt by letting God's kindness flow through me, one simple act at a time.

Notes, Thoughts, and Ideas

ENCOURAGEMENT FOR THE WEEK AHEAD

The weight of anxiety often makes us focus inward, yet healing often comes when we look outward in love. You don't need to solve the world's brokenness all at once. Just start with the person in front of you. A kind word, a patient response, a moment of genuine listening—these seemingly small gestures carry the very heart of Christ to a wounded world. When anxiety makes you feel powerless, remember that kindness is always within your reach. Each compassionate choice creates a ripple that extends far beyond what you can see. By choosing love over hurt, you become part of God's healing work in this broken world.

Week 25: Beyond Fair Weather

"A friend loves at all times."

(PROVERBS 17:17)

When things are easy or fun, life's a crowd. When life gets tough, few true friends show up. Something you may know all too well.

God sends to you a love that endures beyond the fair-weather moments. It's the friend who stays when the storms come, who listens when you're hurting, and who prays for you when you feel weak.

As He blesses you with this kind of friend, you, too, can be that. Loving at all times means showing up when it's not convenient, offering grace when mistakes are made, and being a constant source of encouragement. It's not always about big gestures but small, meaningful acts—like a phone call when they're feeling lonely or offering help without being asked.

Remain faithful to them through their flaws and failures. Just as Jesus does to you. By His love overflowing in you, seek to be a friend who stays and carries each other through both the sunny and stormy days of life.

A Prayer in Times of Anxiety

Lord, thank You for sending friends who stay when life gets tough. When anxiety makes me feel alone, remind me of those who've shown me Your enduring love through their presence. Help me be that kind of friend too— the one who shows up, listens, and prays. Give me the strength to love others through their storms as You have loved me through mine. When it's not convenient or easy, help me remember Your faithfulness to me despite my flaws. May Your love overflow from me to others. Amen.

STILLING THE STORM WITHIN

Who has God placed in my life as a true friend who stays during the storms, and how have they reflected Christ's love to me?

In what ways might my anxiety be preventing me from being fully present for others when they're struggling?

How can I show up in small, meaningful ways for someone who needs a faithful friend right now?

Anxiety Release Affirmation

Christ's faithful love empowers me to be a true friend who stays present in both sunny days and stormy seasons.

Notes, Thoughts, and Ideas

ENCOURAGEMENT FOR THE WEEK AHEAD

Anxiety often tells us we're isolated in our struggles, but God weaves faithful friends into the fabric of our lives to prove otherwise. These relationships aren't just nice additions to your life—they're sacred mirrors reflecting God's unwavering commitment to you. When you choose to be present in someone else's pain, you're offering them more than companionship; you're showing them the heart of Jesus.

The next time anxiety makes you want to withdraw, remember that your presence in someone's storm might be exactly what helps them weather it. Each time you choose to stay when it would be easier to leave, you participate in God's enduring love.

Week 26: Shared Pilgrimage

*"Rejoice with those who rejoice;
mourn with those who mourn."*

(ROMANS 12:15)

You cherish the ones who celebrate you for your efforts, and with them, small wins are significant. They, too, are the ones who sense your troubled spirit and sit with you in silence when the sorrow is beyond words. They are your kindred spirits.

God's children are called to walk alongside one another, to the peak, to the pit, and through the plain path. It takes a compassionate heart to truly share in someone else's happiness or pain.

The key is to love and walk faithfully wherever God sends you. It's an act of love to genuinely feel another's joy as if it were your own. It's also love to ache deeply for another's grief.

But how can others walk with you if you keep hiding? How can they know you if you don't let them in? Too many others live alone.

Brave the walls and share your pilgrimage.

A Prayer in Times of Anxiety

Father, thank You for the kindred spirits You've placed in my life who celebrate my small wins and sit with me in wordless sorrow. When anxiety makes me build walls, give me courage to let others in. Help me be vulnerable enough to share both my joys and struggles. Thank You for calling us to walk together—to peaks, pits, and plains. Teach me to both receive and give this gift of faithful companionship. Help me brave the walls that keep me isolated and share my true journey with others. Amen.

STILLING THE STORM WITHIN

What walls have I built that prevent others from truly walking alongside me in my anxiety?

How might my reluctance to be vulnerable be robbing both myself and others of the community God intended?

What small step could I take today to let someone into my real struggles rather than presenting only my polished self?

Anxiety Release Affirmation

God designed me for authentic community, and sharing my journey honestly opens the door to healing connection.

Notes, Thoughts, and Ideas

ENCOURAGEMENT FOR THE WEEK AHEAD

Anxiety thrives in isolation, building walls brick by brick until you're surrounded by a fortress of your own making. But those walls that seem to protect you actually imprison you. The people God has placed in your life can't walk with you if they can't find you. Your vulnerability isn't weakness—it's the bridge that allows true connection to happen. When you brave those walls and let others see your real journey, you create space for genuine healing. The next time anxiety tells you to hide, remember that someone else may be waiting for permission to be real too. Your courage might be exactly what they need to find their own.

Week 27: Even in the Tunnel

"Do not fear, for I am with you; do not be dismayed, for I am your God."

(ISAIAH 41:10)

You've been bravely holding onto your threads of faith for so long. But now your strength is wavering, and perseverance feels almost impossible. You wonder if continuing to hold on even makes sense anymore or if you're just setting yourself up for deeper disappointment in the end.

That's the way it is when you walk or even crawl along a tunnel. The darkness confuses you, at the very least. You know you wouldn't want to settle there, but it makes you doubt if you possess the strength to make it through. It also makes you forget that God walks alongside you there.

In His tender mercies, God speaks to your very fear. He gently and patiently nudges you to bring you to the reassurance that He never leaves you on your own. Such is God—ever faithful and ever loving. You can be still now, confident that He will bring you to the end of the tunnel. Throughout, He is your light and might.

A Prayer in Times of Anxiety

Lord, in my moments of darkness and doubt, when I wonder if holding on makes sense, remind me of Your faithful presence. When anxiety clouds my vision and my strength wavers, help me remember You walk alongside me. Thank You that even when I can only crawl, You are my light and might. I surrender my fears and worries to You, trusting Your tender mercies to guide me through. Amen.

STILLING THE STORM WITHIN

How has God shown His faithfulness to you during your most difficult moments of anxiety or doubt?

In what specific "tunnels" of your life do you need to be reminded that God is walking alongside you right now?

What practical step can you take today to be still and trust that God will bring you through your current struggles?

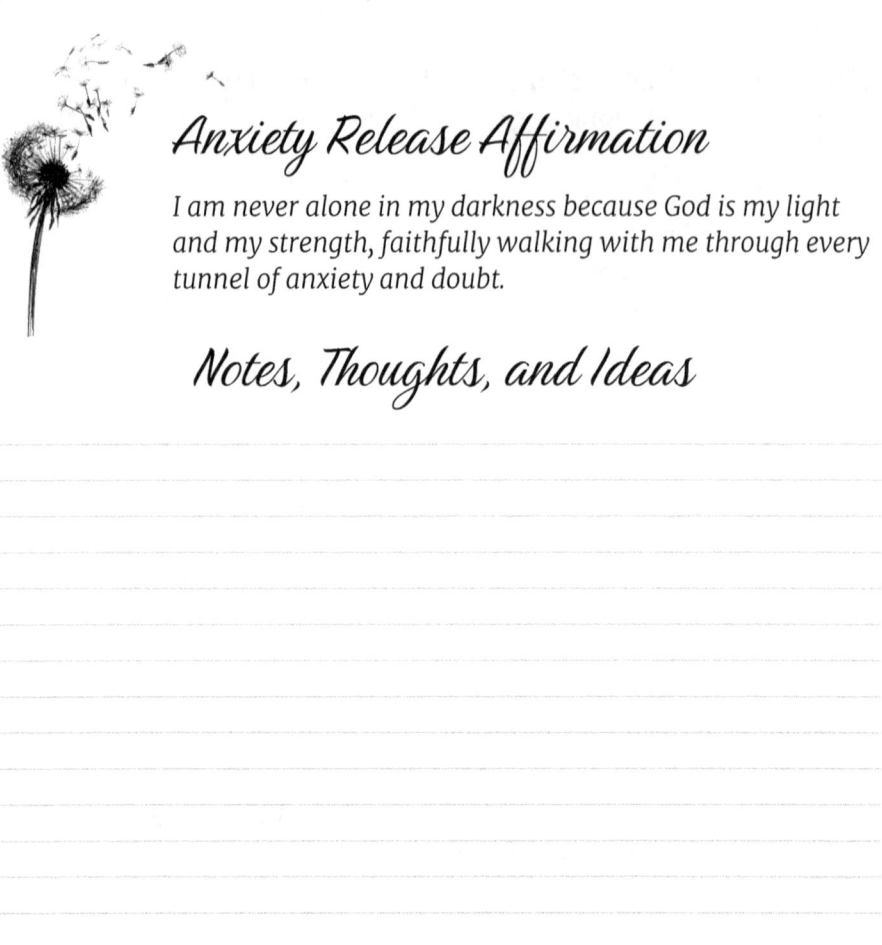

Anxiety Release Affirmation

I am never alone in my darkness because God is my light and my strength, faithfully walking with me through every tunnel of anxiety and doubt.

Notes, Thoughts, and Ideas

ENCOURAGEMENT FOR THE WEEK AHEAD

The path through anxiety is rarely a straight line. Some days you'll stride forward confidently; other days you'll only manage to crawl. Both are progress. Both are part of the journey God walks with you. Remember that your doubt doesn't diminish His faithfulness, and your fear doesn't drive Him away. He meets you in the middle of your questions, your weariness, and your struggle to hold on—not just after you've found the answers.

His light doesn't always show you the entire path, but it always shows you the next step. And sometimes, that next step is simply being still and knowing He is God, present and active in your darkness.

Week 28: My True Portrait

"Do not fear, for I am with you; do not be dismayed, for I am your God."

(ISAIAH 41:10)

Some days you think you are God's masterpiece. On other days, you would question if that were true because you feel like you were a mistake. And it adds to the sinking of your heart to think that maybe your life was overlooked by the Creator.

So for the days you may feel lost or unsure, this verse is a beautiful assurance about your person and purpose, too.

The Word of Truth tells this about your redemption in Christ, along with the grander picture of God's plan, in which you are called to take part. He mindfully made you, united you to His Son, and all your days together.

As you face each day, you don't walk aimlessly. Jesus directs your every moment with grace. He has intricately woven His plans for you into the fabric of your life, guiding your steps with love and wisdom. You can live in the honor of displaying the goodness of Christ in your life!

A Prayer in Times of Anxiety

Father, on days when I question my worth and purpose, when anxious thoughts make me feel like a mistake rather than Your masterpiece, draw me back to Your truth. Thank You for mindfully creating me and uniting me with Christ. Help me see myself through Your eyes—as someone designed with purpose and love. When I feel lost, remind me that You've already mapped my journey with grace. May I find peace in knowing I'm never overlooked by You. Amen.

STILLING THE STORM WITHIN

How might viewing yourself as God's masterpiece change the way you approach your struggles with anxiety?

What "good works" might God be preparing for you to do, even in the midst of your current struggles with worry?

In what specific ways can you practice seeing yourself through God's eyes rather than through the lens of anxiety?

Anxiety Release Affirmation

I am God's masterpiece, intentionally created and united with Christ, with a divine purpose that anxiety cannot diminish.

Notes, Thoughts, and Ideas

ENCOURAGEMENT FOR THE WEEK AHEAD

The battle between knowing you're God's masterpiece and feeling like a mistake is one that many of us face, especially in moments of anxiety. Remember that your worth isn't determined by your feelings but by God's unchanging truth. On days when you feel overlooked or purposeless, pause and recall that the Creator of the universe designed you with intention. Your anxiety doesn't define you—your identity in Christ does. Each step, even through worry and doubt, is part of the intricate plan He's weaving. You're never aimless, never forgotten, never a mistake. Walk forward today, not in perfect confidence perhaps, but in the perfect love of the One who calls you His masterpiece.

Week 29: To Win the War

"The Lord will fight for you; you need only to be still."

(EXODUS 14:14)

The battles rage, and there are some that you win. Though more are lost. As your strength wanes, you look ahead, resigned to the fact that this war will not be victorious.

This was how the Israelites felt.

They were being chased by their Egyptian enemies, who were closing in. The desert was behind them and the Red Sea was in front of them. It seemed like wherever they went, destruction was their fate. But they went the faith way.

The Almighty stands ever victorious, and He comes to wage war for you! The enemies will ultimately be slain as you await in stillness for His great display of deliverance. But the key is to realize this war wasn't yours to fight against. This war is for God's glory, so He Himself is in command. So when every way seems a step to defeat, look with eyes of faith that you were meant to win this with God!

A Prayer in Times of Anxiety

Lord, when my battles overwhelm me and defeat seems inevitable, when anxiety closes in from all sides like the Egyptians pursuing Your people, help me remember that this war isn't mine to fight alone. In these moments when I see no way forward, teach me to be still and trust Your command. Thank You that You stand ever victorious and fight for me when my strength fails. Give me eyes of faith to see Your deliverance even before it appears. I surrender my anxiety to Your mighty hands. Amen.

STILLING THE STORM WITHIN

Where in your life do you feel trapped between "the desert and the sea," with anxiety pressing in and no clear path forward?

How might waiting in stillness, rather than frantic action, change your experience of anxiety moving forward?

What would it look like for you to truly believe that God fights for you in the battles that seem unwinnable?

Anxiety Release Affirmation

The battles that overwhelm me are under God's command, and through His strength, not mine, victory is already secured.

Notes, Thoughts, and Ideas

ENCOURAGEMENT FOR THE WEEK AHEAD

Anxiety often feels like being caught between impossible options—trapped with enemies closing in and no escape route in sight. But God specializes in impossible situations. When you've exhausted your strategies and your strength has failed, that's precisely when His power is most perfectly displayed. The stillness He calls you to isn't passive resignation but active trust—a declaration that you know Who controls the outcome. Your anxiety doesn't have the final word. Your limitations don't determine the result. God fights for you with resources you cannot see and power you cannot imagine. Today, in whatever battle you face, take a deep breath and stand still. Watch for His deliverance. It's coming.

Week 30: He Meets You More Than Halfway

"The Lord your God is with you, the Mighty Warrior who saves. He will take great delight in you; in his love, he will no longer rebuke you but will rejoice over you with singing."

(ZEPHANIAH 3:17)

When you've done everything you can and still come up short, it's beyond frustrating. You question your ability. Then you dwell in your inadequacy. But you're not the only one who makes prayer the last resort. Yes, the very thing you thought and dismissed as ineffective.

It is not the prayers that can lift you from your situation. It is the God to whom you pray. He is more than able to save you. As the Father whose life is in His child, He delights in you with heavenly joy, affection, and singing. He knows every detail of your life and the grand scheme of the universe. He awaits just one step from you to draw near to Him, and then He travels all the way to meet you.

That one step is to call to Him in prayer. He knows your faith in Him and love for Him, well more than you know. He also sees your need for Him, so He shows you His heart that you may let Him help you. What a Savior He is, truly the Lover of your soul! Just a step to songs of deliverance!

A Prayer in Times of Anxiety

Heavenly Father, when anxiety has me in its grip and my own efforts leave me exhausted and still coming up short, forgive me for making prayer my last resort. In these moments of frustration and inadequacy, remind me that You await just one step toward You. Thank You that You don't stand distant but run to meet me, delighting in me with joy and singing over me with love. Help me turn to You first, not last, knowing that in Your presence, my anxious heart finds true peace. Amen.

STILLING THE STORM WITHIN

How might your experience of anxiety change if you made prayer your first response rather than your last resort?

What keeps you from taking that one step toward God when you feel overwhelmed and inadequate?

In what specific situation do you need to stop striving in your own strength and instead call out to the God who delights in you?

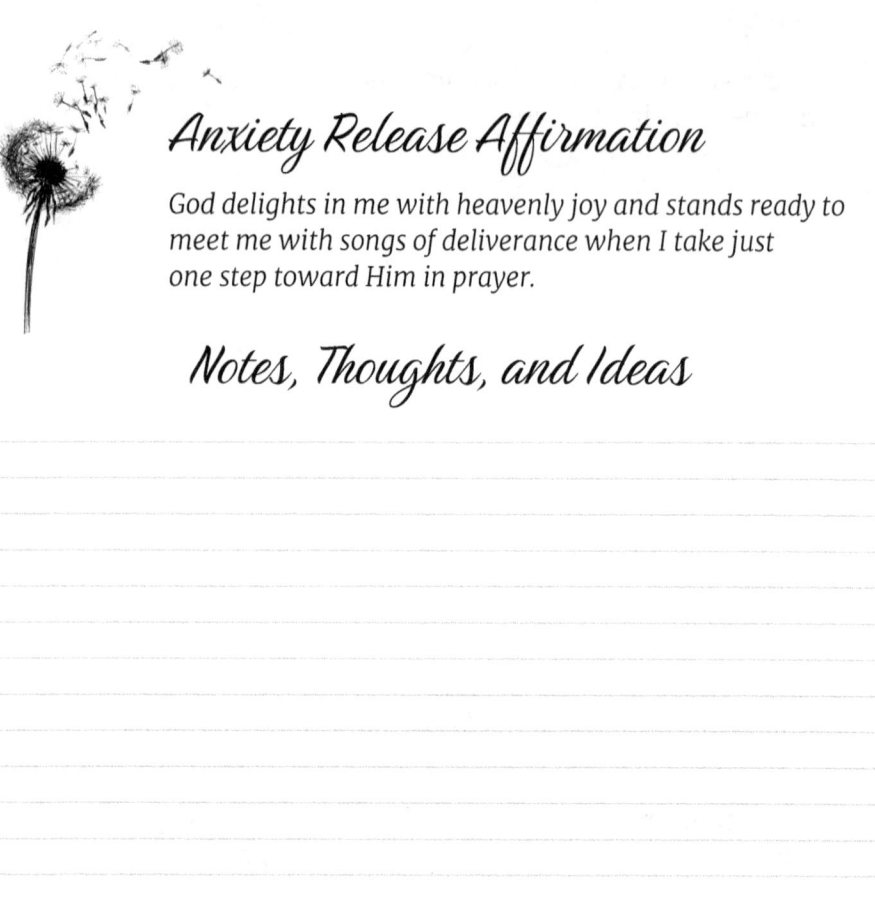

Anxiety Release Affirmation

God delights in me with heavenly joy and stands ready to meet me with songs of deliverance when I take just one step toward Him in prayer.

Notes, Thoughts, and Ideas

ENCOURAGEMENT FOR THE WEEK AHEAD

Anxiety tricks us into believing we must solve everything ourselves, that prayer is somehow less practical than our frantic efforts. But what if the most practical thing you could do is pause and remember who God is? He's not a distant deity who needs convincing to care—He's a Father who sings over you, delights in you, and knows every detail of your struggle. Your inadequacy isn't news to Him; it's precisely where His strength shines brightest. When anxiety has you questioning everything about yourself, stop and take that one step. Call out to Him. Not because prayer is magical, but because the God who hears you is mighty. Your anxiety doesn't intimidate Him; your weakness doesn't disappoint Him. He's waiting, ready to travel all the way to where you are.

Week 31: A New Friend

*"When you pass through the waters,
I will be with you; and when you pass through the rivers,
they will not sweep over you."*

(ISAIAH 43:2)

You keep your head afloat, but the water just keeps rising too. And when you think you've mastered the still water, the mighty currents come. The struggle just will not stop!

God says, let even the waves come! None can drown you. You will sail through and see that all the water is His servant, helping you be brought near to Him. This mindset will still your doubts and fears. The water is your friend, as it is God's instrument to bless you. So even when you feel everything surrounding you is too much, your anchor is God, the One who is unshakeable and unchangeable!

When you're tossed around and tired, don't be afraid of where life will take you. The hands of God are keeping you safe and embracing you. Reject the lie that you are drowning. Smile in the sweet assurance that the Lifeguard swims with you. Enjoy the water and sail through assuredly.

A Prayer in Times of Anxiety

Father, when anxiety rises like water around me and each new wave threatens to pull me under, help me remember that even these waves are Your servants. In moments when I'm gasping for breath, struggling to stay afloat in my worries, remind me that You are my unshakeable anchor. Thank You that I don't swim alone—the divine Lifeguard is always with me. Give me courage to see these waters not as my enemy but as Your instrument bringing me closer to You. Help me sail through with confidence in Your embrace. Amen.

STILLING THE STORM WITHIN

How might your response to anxiety change if you viewed your struggles as God's instruments to draw you closer to Him?

_____
_____
_____
_____
_____
_____
_____
_____
_____
_____
_____
_____
_____
_____
_____

Where in your life do you need to stop fighting against the "water" and instead trust that God is using it for your good?

What lies about "drowning" in anxiety do you need to reject today, and how can you replace them with truths about God's presence with you?

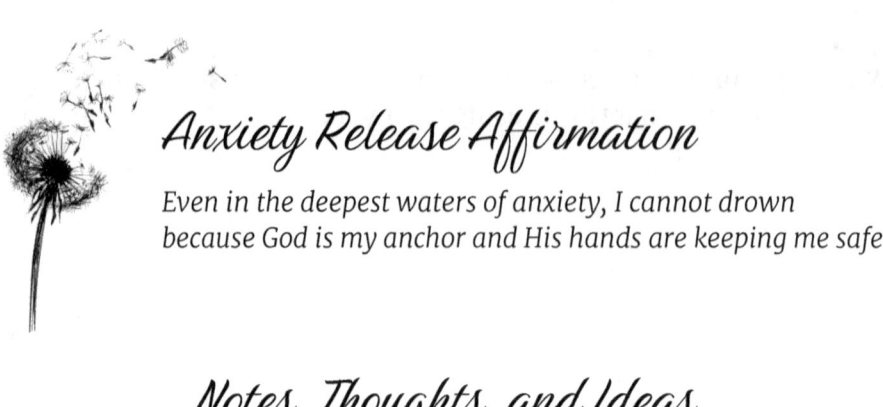

Anxiety Release Affirmation

Even in the deepest waters of anxiety, I cannot drown because God is my anchor and His hands are keeping me safe

Notes, Thoughts, and Ideas

ENCOURAGEMENT FOR THE WEEK AHEAD

The panic of feeling like you're drowning in anxiety is real. Your lungs burn, your limbs tire, and the surface seems impossibly far away. But what if this water isn't your enemy? What if these very waves that terrify you are actually carrying you somewhere better? God doesn't promise still waters always, but He does promise His presence in every current. When you're tired of treading water and fighting the tide, perhaps the bravest thing is to release your exhausted struggle and trust the flow. Not because you've given up, but because you've given over to the One who commands even the storms. You were never meant to master the water alone. You were meant to discover that in your deepest need, you are most powerfully held.

Week 32: Known Fully

*"The Lord is close to the brokenhearted
and saves those who are crushed in spirit."*

(PSALM 34:18)

When life feels heavy, trying to explain how you are makes it even heavier. Finding the words can drain the life out of you. Trying to make others understand you feels too exhausting. Can't anyone know you in your silence?

God alone does.

In those moments when you feel overwhelmed, hurt, or alone, remember this truth: God is near. He understands your heartache, your struggles, and your fears. He isn't distant or detached; He is right there with you, walking alongside you in your pain. So even when you don't tell Him anything, He gets you completely.

God's presence is a comfort. He draws near to those who are hurting, and this is more than enough. His love and care are always available, and He is ready to carry your burdens. Trust that He is ever close, that He is holding you, and that He will heal your brokenness in His perfect time.

A Prayer in Times of Anxiety

Lord, in these silent moments when words fail me and anxiety steals my voice, thank You for knowing me completely. When explaining my pain to others feels impossible and loneliness weighs heavy on my heart, I'm grateful You understand without my having to form a single sentence. Thank You for being near when I feel overwhelmed, hurt, and alone. Help me rest in the comfort of Your presence when life drains me of words and energy. Remind me that being known by You is enough, even in my silence. Amen.

STILLING THE STORM WITHIN

How does knowing that God understands you even in your wordless moments change how you experience anxiety?

When have you felt God's presence most clearly during times when you couldn't explain your feelings to others?

What burdens are you carrying today that you need to entrust to God's care?

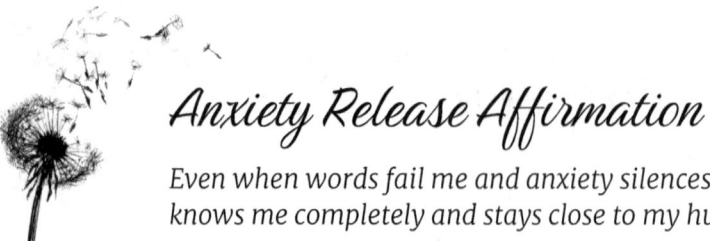

Anxiety Release Affirmation

Even when words fail me and anxiety silences my voice, God knows me completely and stays close to my hurting heart.

Notes, Thoughts, and Ideas

ENCOURAGEMENT FOR THE WEEK AHEAD

There's a special kind of exhaustion that comes from trying to translate your inner world for others—explaining anxiety to someone who hasn't felt it can deplete what little energy you have left. But with God, you don't need to find the right words. You don't need to make your pain sound reasonable or your fears justified. He knows. He sees. And He stays. When the weight of being understood becomes too much, let yourself rest in the quiet comfort of being fully known. Your silent tears speak volumes to Him. Your wordless sighs are prayers He perfectly interprets. You don't have to carry the double burden of feeling pain and then explaining that pain. Simply be still and know that He is God—and that His knowing you is healing in itself.

Week 33: Neither Alone nor Lonely

"Take my yoke upon you and learn from me, for I am gentle and humble in heart, and you will find rest for your souls. For my yoke is easy and my burden is light."

(MATTHEW 11:29-30)

Life is difficult as it is. Suffering from the loneliness anxiety causes can worsen it. Yet other people can make it doubly challenging, so you would rather deal with life alone.

Jesus, however, is trustworthy. He doesn't ask you to walk through life alone or bear your struggles in isolation. Instead, He offers Himself as your faithful partner.

When you feel weighed down by responsibilities, worries, or hardships, remember that Jesus is right there beside you, ready to share the load. He doesn't just give you a task and walk away; He comes alongside you, helping you navigate through the challenges. His yoke is not harsh or burdensome—His presence makes even the heaviest loads lighter. So, take a deep breath and let go of the pressure to do everything on your own. Jesus is your loving partner, offering you rest, peace, and the strength to keep moving forward. With Him, you don't have to carry it all alone.

A Prayer in Times of Anxiety

Jesus, when anxiety isolates me and makes the world feel too overwhelming to face, thank You for Your invitation to walk with You. When I'm tempted to retreat and handle everything alone, remind me that Your yoke connects us. Thank You for being gentle with my fragile heart and humble enough to meet me in my mess. I surrender my loneliness, my worries, and my burdens to You today. Help me feel the lightness that comes from sharing this journey with You, knowing I am neither alone nor truly lonely with You by my side. Amen.

STILLING THE STORM WITHIN

How has trying to handle anxiety on your own affected your relationship with others and with God?

What specific burdens feel too heavy right now that you need to consciously place under Jesus' yoke?

What would it look like in your daily life to truly accept Jesus' offer to be your partner in carrying your anxieties?

Anxiety Release Affirmation

I am never truly alone because Jesus walks beside me, making my heaviest burdens lighter through His gentle and humble partnership.

Notes, Thoughts, and Ideas

ENCOURAGEMENT FOR THE WEEK AHEAD

Anxiety has a way of building walls around us—convincing us that no one understands, that we're safer handling things alone, that vulnerability is dangerous. But those walls that seem to protect us often become our prison. Jesus doesn't force His way through them; He gently invites you to open the door. Partnership with Him doesn't mean your troubles instantly vanish, but it does mean you never face them isolated and overwhelmed. When anxiety whispers "retreat," remember that the One who calmed the storm knows exactly how to calm your heart. His yoke isn't another burden—it's the connection that transforms your solitary struggle into a supported journey. You were never meant to carry life alone. Take His hand today.

Week 34: The True and Worthy You

"I am fearfully and wonderfully made"

(PSALM 139:14)

Sometimes, it's easy to fall into the trap of comparing yourself to others or feeling like you don't measure up. The world sets the standards and defines what people ought to be. And how they favor the few at the expense of many others, most tragically neglecting the souls of people.

If you've ever struggled with feelings of unworthiness, know that this verse is a beautiful reminder of your true value. God created you with purpose, intricacy, and love. Every part of you, even the parts you wish were different, is a masterpiece in His eyes.

By the grace of God in Jesus Christ, you are restored to be who you truly are, as originally designed in creation. The person who is very good and who gives glory to His Creator. That person, who you truly are, is the person you are in Jesus Christ.

So, when feelings of unworthiness creep in, remind yourself of God's truth: you are fearfully and wonderfully made. You are worthy, not because of anything you've done, but because of who you are in Christ.

A Prayer in Times of Anxiety

Father, when anxiety makes me question my worth and I fall into the trap of comparing myself to others, remind me of Your truth. Thank You for creating me fearfully and wonderfully, with purpose and love. When the world's standards make me feel inadequate, help me see myself through Your eyes. Thank You that in Christ, I am restored to who You designed me to be. In moments when I feel unworthy or not enough, whisper Your affirmation over me. Help me embrace the true and worthy person You created me to be, finding my identity in You alone. Amen.

STILLING THE STORM WITHIN

How has comparing yourself to others contributed to your anxiety, and what truth from Psalm 139 speaks directly to that comparison?

What parts of yourself do you struggle to see as "wonderfully made," and how might viewing them through God's eyes change your perspective?

What would look different in your daily life if you truly lived from the identity of being restored in Christ rather than from feelings of unworthiness?

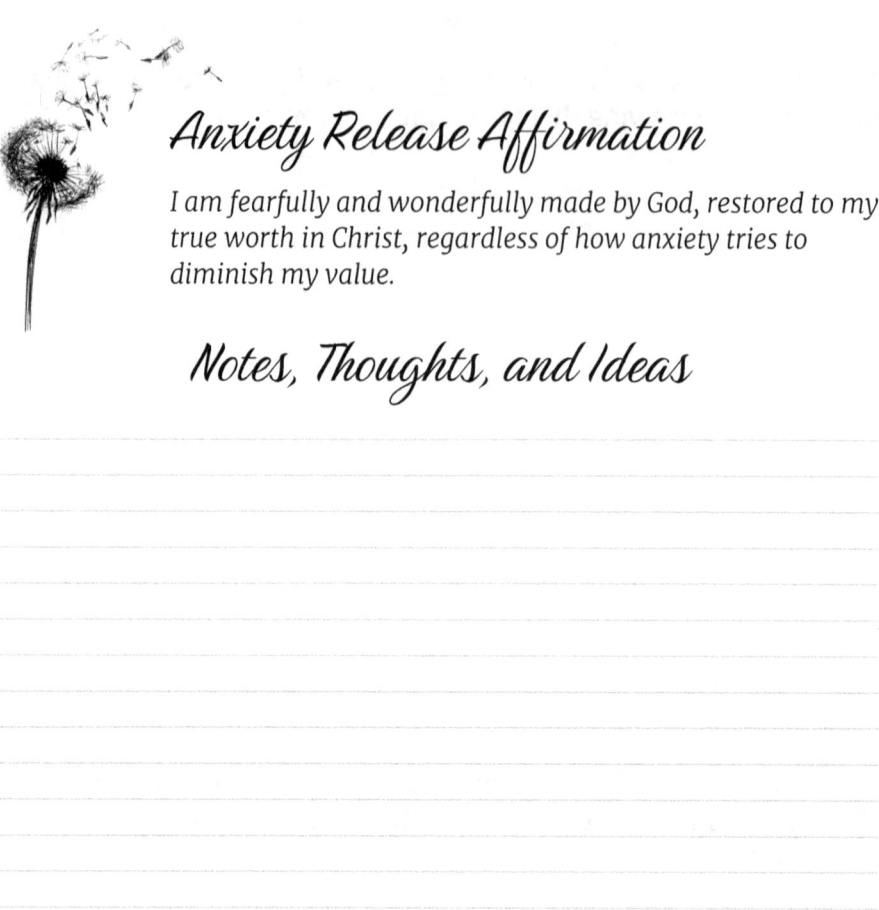

Anxiety Release Affirmation

I am fearfully and wonderfully made by God, restored to my true worth in Christ, regardless of how anxiety tries to diminish my value.

Notes, Thoughts, and Ideas

ENCOURAGEMENT FOR THE WEEK AHEAD

The voices of unworthiness are loud in our anxious world. They shout from billboards, whisper through social media, and echo in casual conversations that somehow leave us feeling less than. But there's an older voice, a truer voice that speaks your name with tenderness and precision. The One who knit you together sees no mistake in His handiwork. Your worth was never meant to be measured against others or earned through performance. It was established the moment God breathed life into you and sealed when Christ gave His life for you. When anxiety tells you that you don't measure up, remember that you were never meant to fit the world's mold—you were created to reflect the image of God in a way only you can.

Week 35: Strong as Paul

"I can do all this through him who gives me strength."

(PHILIPPIANS 4:13)

You think to yourself that others make it through because they're strong, unlike you. Life would be so much better if you were not weak. But the Word of God reveals how you can powerfully make it.

When Paul wrote this, he was in prison, facing hardship and uncertainty. Yet, he didn't see his circumstances as limitations. Instead, he recognized that his strength came from Christ, not his own abilities. Whether in abundance or need, Paul found contentment in Jesus, knowing that God's power was enough to carry him through any situation.

Today, this verse speaks to you just as powerfully. Life can bring unexpected challenges—financial struggles, emotional burdens, or moments of doubt. Like Paul, you can face these difficulties with the assurance that Christ is with you, strengthening you. He doesn't promise an easy life, but He does promise to empower you to rise above every circumstance. His strength is sufficient for you today, just as it was for Paul.

A Prayer in Times of Anxiety

Heavenly Father, thank You for making Your power perfect in my weakness. When anxiety overwhelms me, help me remember these moments reveal Your strength working through me. Thank You for being my sufficiency in every circumstance. Fill me with peace knowing Your power empowers me to face each challenge. In Christ, I have all I need for whatever lies ahead. Amen.

STILLING THE STORM WITHIN

How has comparing your strength to others affected your experience of anxiety?

When have you seen Christ's strength manifest in your life during a time when you felt particularly weak?

What current situation feels impossible right now that you need to surrender to Christ's strength rather than your own?

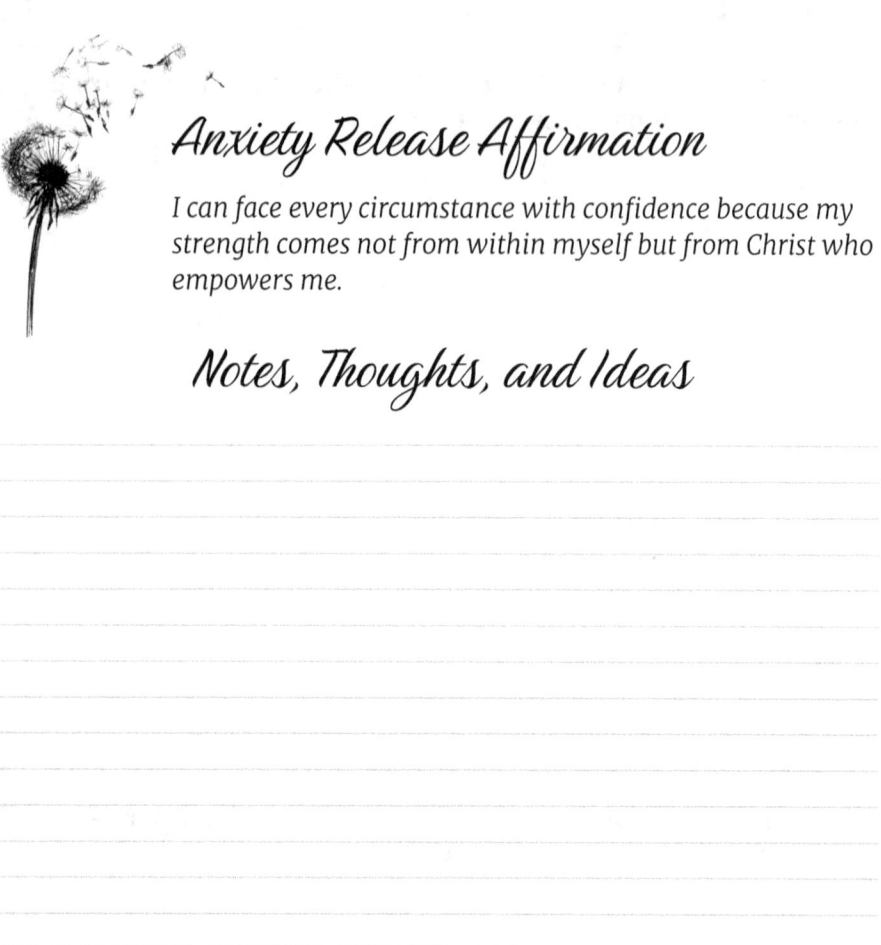

Anxiety Release Affirmation

I can face every circumstance with confidence because my strength comes not from within myself but from Christ who empowers me.

Notes, Thoughts, and Ideas

ENCOURAGEMENT FOR THE WEEK AHEAD

Anxiety often masquerades as truth, whispering that your struggles prove your weakness while others succeed through their strength. But what if the real difference isn't between strength and weakness, but between self-sufficiency and surrender? Paul's secret wasn't superior courage or resilience—it was complete dependence on a power beyond himself. Your anxiety doesn't disqualify you from experiencing this same strength. In fact, it might be the very thing that drives you to the source of true power. Today, your circumstances might not change, your feelings might remain turbulent, and your path forward might still seem unclear. But in Christ, you have access to a strength that doesn't depend on any of those things—a power made perfect precisely in your weakness.

Week 36: Always According to God's Plan

"And we know that in all things God works for the good of those who love him, who have been called according to his purpose."

(ROMANS 8:28)

People rarely experience life unfolding according to their initial plans. At times, it all goes south. Feelings of anxiety become overwhelming when life takes a negative turn because everything seems to be breaking down. But God is always working behind the scenes. He is directing everything for your good, even when you can't see it. It is His plan. Today's setbacks are part of His greater purpose.

Trust that God is doing His work, despite your most difficult challenges. God has a complete understanding of the entire redemption plan, which He fulfills in your lifetime. He's shaping you, refining you, and preparing you for something even more beautiful than you could imagine.

His love and faithfulness are constant, and He's guiding you toward a future filled with His hope and grace. Knowing this goes beyond cerebral. To know this means you choose to keep trusting and awaiting the good that will ultimately result from your life, no matter how bleak the situation is at the moment. All will move according to God's beautiful plan.

A Prayer in Times of Anxiety

Heavenly Father, when anxiety floods my heart as life veers off course, help me remember You're still orchestrating everything. When things seem to be falling apart, give me courage to trust Your unseen work. Thank You for seeing the complete picture when I only see fragments. Quiet my racing thoughts with the assurance of Your love and perfect timing.

Help me choose trust over fear, even when the path ahead seems uncertain. Remind me that today's setbacks are part of tomorrow's redemption story in Your hands. Amen.

STILLING THE STORM WITHIN

How might viewing your current struggles as part of God's greater purpose change your experience of anxiety?

When have you previously seen God work something difficult into something beautiful in your life?

What specific area of uncertainty are you facing now that requires a deeper trust in God's behind-the-scenes work?

Anxiety Release Affirmation

God is faithfully working for my good even in circumstances that trigger my anxiety, orchestrating a future more beautiful than I can imagine.

Notes, Thoughts, and Ideas

ENCOURAGEMENT FOR THE WEEK AHEAD

Anxiety thrives in the gap between our expectations and our reality—that uncomfortable space where plans collapse and uncertainty grows. But what if that gap isn't empty? What if it's actually filled with God's invisible work? Your life's detours aren't random accidents or cruel twists of fate. They're sacred spaces where God shapes your character, deepens your faith, and weaves your story into His redemption narrative. The courage to trust isn't about having all the answers or seeing the complete path ahead. It's about remembering who holds your story and choosing to believe in His goodness even when everything feels wrong. Today's pain may be tomorrow's testimony of His faithfulness. Trust the Author—He hasn't finished writing yet.

Week 37: Rest for the Mind

"You will keep in perfect peace those whose minds are steadfast because they trust in you. Trust in the Lord forever, for the Lord, the Lord himself, is the Rock eternal."

(ISAIAH 26:3-4)

It's easy for your mind to become restless, filled with worries and distractions. But God offers you peace—perfect peace—when you keep your mind focused on Him. To be steadfast means to remain firm and unwavering, and when you trust in the Lord, He strengthens your heart and mind to do just that. As you focus on His faithfulness, He guards your heart from worry, offering a peace that transcends understanding.

When the world feels unstable, the Lord is your Rock eternal—unchanging, firm, and reliable. He is the foundation that doesn't shift with circumstances. As you trust in Him, you find a peace that doesn't depend on what's happening around you but on who He is.

The enemy wills all he can to distract you and then steal your peace. So, today, set your mind on Jesus. Trust in Him, and let His peace fill your soul.

A Prayer in Times of Anxiety

Lord, when my mind races with worries and my thoughts scatter in a thousand directions, draw me back to You. In these moments when anxiety threatens to overwhelm me, help me fix my eyes on Your unchanging nature. Thank You for being my Rock eternal when everything else feels unstable. Quiet the noise in my mind and replace it with Your perfect peace. When the enemy tries to steal my focus and my peace, strengthen my resolve to remain steadfast in trusting You. Help me set my mind on Jesus today and every day, finding rest in Your unwavering presence. Amen.

STILLING THE STORM WITHIN

What specific worries or distractions most easily pull your mind away from focusing on God?

How have you experienced God's peace in past situations when you deliberately chose to trust Him despite your anxiety?

What practical steps can you take today to set your mind on Jesus when anxious thoughts begin to intrude?

Anxiety Release Affirmation

As I keep my mind steadfastly focused on God rather than my anxieties, His perfect peace guards my heart and mind in all circumstances.

Notes, Thoughts, and Ideas

ENCOURAGEMENT FOR THE WEEK AHEAD

Peace isn't the absence of trouble but the presence of God in the midst of it. When anxiety clouds your vision and your thoughts feel like a storm you can't control, remember that your Rock doesn't move. The steadiness you seek isn't found in perfect circumstances or in having all the answers—it's found in knowing the One who holds all things together. Your mind will always follow what you focus on. When you fix your gaze on problems, they grow larger; when you focus on fears, they multiply. But when you deliberately turn your attention to Jesus, even the biggest worries begin to shrink in the light of who He is. Choose today where your mind will dwell.

Week 38: Trying and Transforming

"Consider it pure joy, my brothers and sisters, whenever you face trials of many kinds, because you know that the testing of your faith produces perseverance. Let perseverance finish its work so that you may be mature and complete, not lacking anything."

(JAMES 1:2-4)

In moments of senseless pain and tragedy, it's natural to feel lost. You live in a broken world where sin, illness, and injustice often seem to cause untold pain. But in the midst of that, you can find solace in knowing that God does not cause or delight in suffering.

Instead, He calls you to consider all joy. This can feel hard to embrace. But the joy James speaks of isn't about celebrating the difficulty itself—it's about recognizing that God is using it to strengthen you.

When you face trials, remember that God is with you, shaping your character and deepening your faith. The challenges you encounter have a purpose. As you endure, you build perseverance—a strength that allows you to handle even greater challenges ahead. This attitude doesn't come easily, but as you rely on God, it transforms you.

So, even in hard times, choose joy, knowing that God is refining you and making you more like Him.

A Prayer in Times of Anxiety

God of all comfort, when anxiety overwhelms me and life's trials feel senseless, help me find the courage to consider it joy. Not because suffering itself is good, but because You work through it all. When my heart is heavy with pain and my mind cannot make sense of what I'm facing, remind me of Your faithful presence. Thank You for walking with me through every valley, using even my darkest moments to shape me. Give me eyes to see beyond my immediate suffering to the perseverance being built within me. Help me choose joy not based on circumstances but on Your unchanging character and purpose. Amen.

STILLING THE STORM WITHIN

How has God used difficult situations in your past to build character and strength you wouldn't have developed otherwise?

_____
_____
_____
_____
_____
_____
_____
_____
_____
_____
_____
_____
_____
_____
_____

What current challenge in your life feels meaningless that you could reframe as an opportunity for growth?

When anxiety feels overwhelming, what specific truth about God's character helps you most in finding joy amid the struggle?

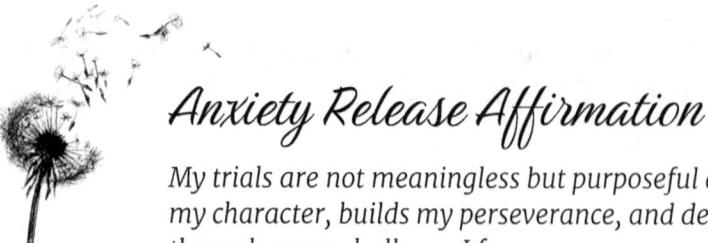

Anxiety Release Affirmation

My trials are not meaningless but purposeful as God shapes my character, builds my perseverance, and deepens my faith through every challenge I face.

Notes, Thoughts, and Ideas

_____
_____
_____
_____
_____
_____
_____
_____
_____
_____
_____
_____
_____

ENCOURAGEMENT FOR THE WEEK AHEAD

The call to find joy in suffering isn't a command to deny your pain or paste on a smile through tears. It's an invitation to see beyond what is happening to what God is doing. Anxiety often stems from feeling that pain has no purpose—that we suffer randomly in a chaotic world. But what if every trial is actually a workshop where God is crafting something beautiful in you? Your anxiety doesn't surprise Him or derail His plans. Instead, He weaves it into His redemptive work, using even your darkest moments to develop steadiness, compassion, and wisdom that couldn't grow any other way. Today, your joy might simply be the quiet acknowledgment that God wastes nothing—not even this.

Week 39: Common and Communal Peace

"Finally, brothers and sisters, rejoice! Strive for full restoration, encourage one another, be of one mind, live in peace. And the God of love and peace will be with you."

(2 CORINTHIANS 13:11)

In the chaos of life, peace can feel elusive, like something just beyond reach. But God promises that peace is within your grasp. Peace is also rare in a world full of division, and God calls you to bridge others.

When you live in harmony with God, peace naturally follows. It's a peace that doesn't depend on perfect circumstances but on His steadfast love for you, which overflows to others. You can make a difference by encouraging others, fostering unity, and promoting peace. It's easy to get caught up in disagreements or frustrations, but God calls you to rise above, building others up with kindness and understanding.

Even amid struggle, you can lean into God's presence today. Trust that He will fill you with peace, not by your striving, but by His loving and gracious hand. Peace is yours, freely given, always within reach. Be generous with peace with others, too.

A Prayer in Times of Anxiety

Heavenly Father, when anxiety makes peace feel out of reach, draw me back to Your promise of perfect peace. When chaos overwhelms me, help me remember Your peace doesn't depend on perfect circumstances but on Your love. Thank You for offering peace as a gift freely given. Fill me with peace that passes understanding, and help me extend it to others. Make me a bridge-builder, showing Your harmony even in difficult relationships. May Your peace flow through me to all I encounter today. Amen.

STILLING THE STORM WITHIN

How might your anxiety decrease if you truly believed peace was a gift from God rather than something you need to achieve?

In what specific relationship or situation could you be a bridge-builder of peace this week and how?

What practical step can you take today to lean into God's presence when peace feels elusive?

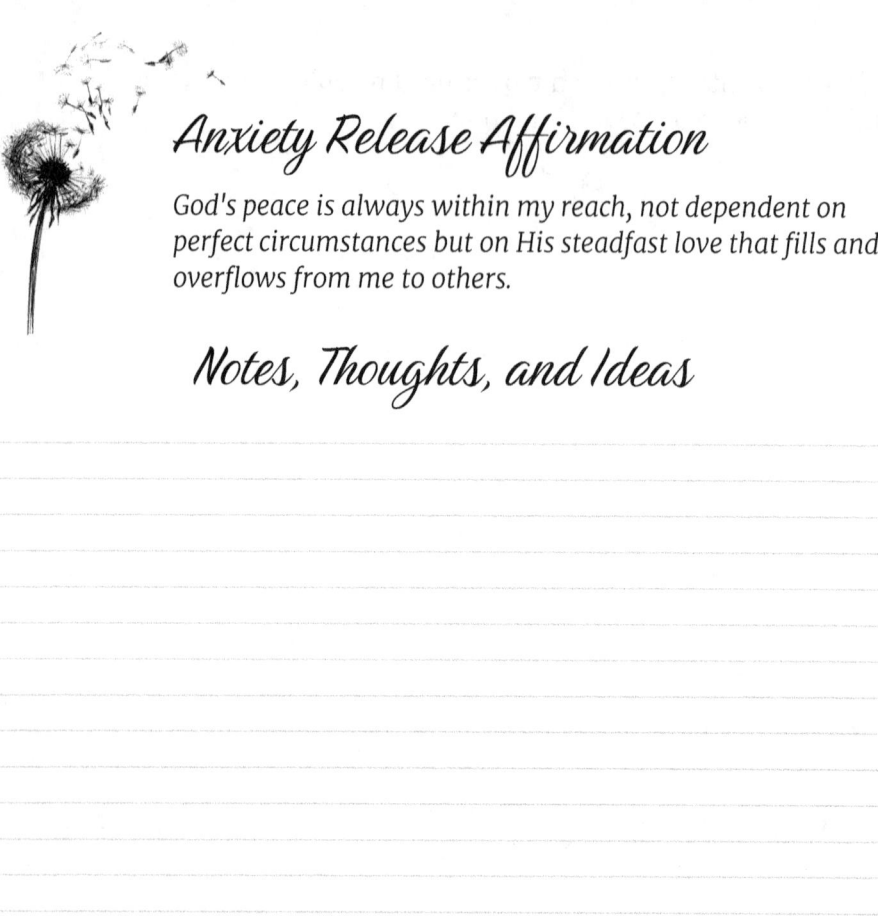

Anxiety Release Affirmation

God's peace is always within my reach, not dependent on perfect circumstances but on His steadfast love that fills and overflows from me to others.

Notes, Thoughts, and Ideas

ENCOURAGEMENT FOR THE WEEK AHEAD

Peace isn't simply the absence of trouble—it's the presence of something greater. When anxiety makes you feel fragmented and scattered, remember that God's peace doesn't arrive once everything is perfect; it arrives in the midst of imperfection. Your role isn't to manufacture peace but to receive it and let it flow through you. Like a river that both refreshes and reshapes the landscape, God's peace can transform how you experience even your most anxious moments. And remarkably, as you receive this peace, you become a channel of it to others. In a world starved for genuine peace, your calm presence—even amid your own struggles—can become the very bridge someone else needs to cross from chaos to comfort.

Week 40: Two-Fold Power

"Be strong and courageous. Do not be afraid or terrified because of them, for the Lord your God goes with you; he will never leave you nor forsake you."

(DEUTERONOMY 31:6)

As a Christian, you face enemies like doubt, fear, temptation, and the pressures of this world. Some days, they knock the wind right out of you. Yet even in those moments, God stands beside you, walking each painful step alongside you. Just as in the days of Joshua when he was entrusted to lead the nation to enter the Promised Land, which was a fortified city and populated by warriors. Such a frightening sight. They wandered too long, and now they are given another chance to trust and obey God by being strong and courageous like they have never done before.

Strength and courage are different, but both are necessary. Strength is the ability to endure and face challenges, while courage is the willingness to take action despite fear. Today you may need both like never before to enter into God's promise for you.

Remember that God doesn't leave you to fight alone. He gives you the strength to endure and the courage to take the steps forward, no matter how daunting. He who promised you gives you the twofold power to possess it!

A Prayer in Times of Anxiety

Lord, when doubt, fear, and anxiety knock the wind out of me, thank You for standing beside me in every painful step. When I feel I've wandered too long in my wilderness, help me see this as another chance to trust You. Thank You that I never face battles alone. Give me strength when anxiety weighs heavy and courage when fear paralyzes me. When my challenges look insurmountable, remind me Your presence makes all the difference. Fill me with endurance and boldness to step into the promises You've prepared for me. Amen.

STILLING THE STORM WITHIN

What specific "fortified walls" in your life cause you the most anxiety right now, and how might God be calling you to face them with His strength?

_____
_____
_____
_____
_____
_____
_____
_____
_____
_____
_____
_____
_____
_____
_____

Where do you need God to show up as your companion in battle right now, and what might that change?

How might your approach to anxiety change if you viewed it as an opportunity to develop both strength (endurance) and courage (action despite fear)?

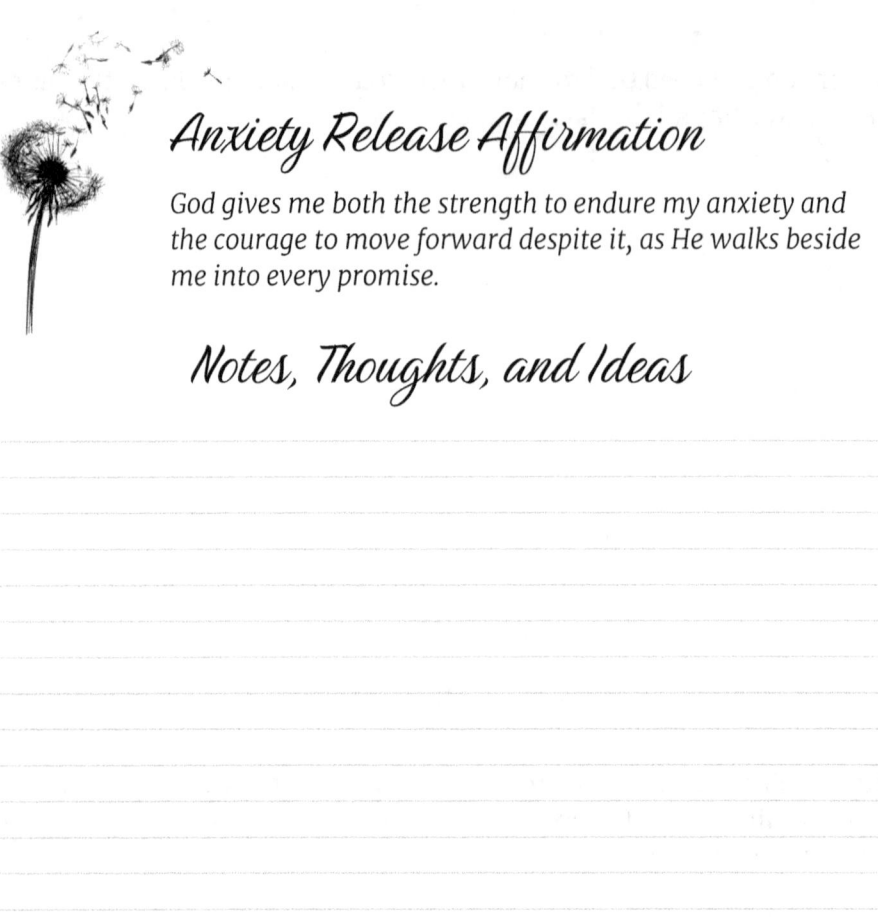

Anxiety Release Affirmation

God gives me both the strength to endure my anxiety and the courage to move forward despite it, as He walks beside me into every promise.

Notes, Thoughts, and Ideas

ENCOURAGEMENT FOR THE WEEK AHEAD

The enemies that assault your peace today might look different from those Joshua faced, but they require the same response: strength and courage that come not from within but from above. Anxiety often makes us forget we're not alone in the battle—that the God who parts waters and crumbles walls stands ready beside us. Your wandering seasons aren't wasted; they're preparation. Your moments of fear aren't failures; they're opportunities to experience God's power in new ways. The promises He's prepared for you may lie just beyond your most fortified fears. Take heart today. The same God who told Joshua "I will never leave you" whispers those words to you now, giving you everything you need to face what lies ahead.

Week 41: Travel Light

"Cast your cares on the Lord and he will sustain you; he will never let the righteous be shaken."

(PSALM 55:22)

Your feelings and fears, your friends and family, your finances and future, your faults and faith, and still more. There is just too much to care about. And they weigh too heavily on your spirit.

With the sheer weight of your burdens, God promises that He will sustain you. And these are not empty words. He truly is ever strong, and He is able to carry the things you cannot lift on your own, especially for a prolonged time.

Your heart will have many cares as you go through life. But you can grow in divine strength to be sustained. When you lay your worries at His feet, He takes them and holds you steady, even when everything around you feels uncertain.

In that moment of surrender, you realize you were truly meant to travel light. And what a joy to see that your cares are not burdensome in God's hands and to experience the lightness of being set free and cared for.

A Prayer in Times of Anxiety

Heavenly Father, when anxiety overwhelms me with too many cares—my feelings, fears, relationships, finances, future, faults, and faith—I come to You with my heavy heart. When worries pile high and weigh down my spirit, help me surrender them completely to Your capable hands. Thank You that what crushes me doesn't even burden You. Remind me that I was created to travel light, with You as my strength. Help me experience the freedom and joy that comes from letting You carry what I cannot. Draw me into Your divine strength today. Amen.

STILLING THE STORM WITHIN

What specific cares and worries are you trying to carry alone right now that you need to intentionally surrender to God?

How might your experience of anxiety change if you truly believed you were "meant to travel light" through life?

When have you felt God sustain you through a difficult time, and what did that teach you about His faithfulness?

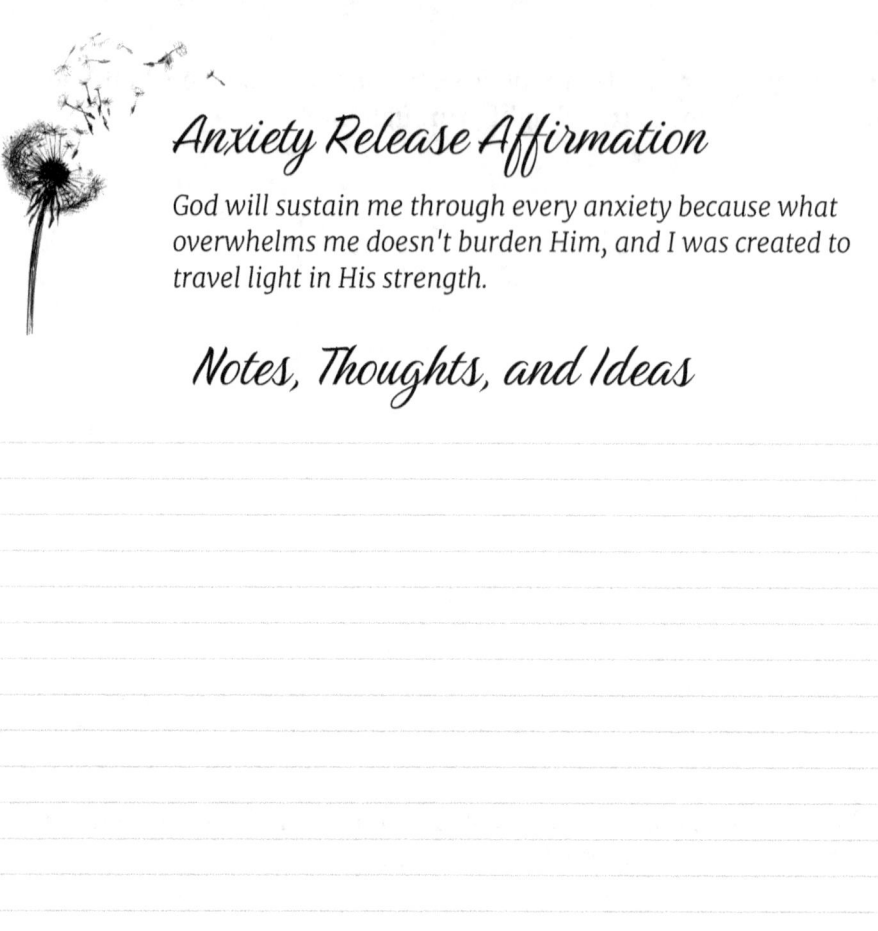

Anxiety Release Affirmation

God will sustain me through every anxiety because what overwhelms me doesn't burden Him, and I was created to travel light in His strength.

Notes, Thoughts, and Ideas

ENCOURAGEMENT FOR THE WEEK AHEAD

The human heart wasn't designed to carry the weight of all our cares. Like trying to carry too many groceries in one trip, we struggle along, dropping things, straining muscles, and arriving exhausted. But God invites us to a different way—not to care less, but to carry differently. When anxiety mounts and your spirit feels crushed beneath its weight, remember that surrender isn't giving up; it's giving over to the One whose strength never fails. The burdens that feel impossible in your hands become manageable in His. The cares that consume your thoughts become opportunities for experiencing His faithfulness. Today, practice the holy art of letting go. Feel the lightness that comes not from having fewer concerns, but from having the right Carrier for them.

Week 42: Walk Side-by-Side

"As iron sharpens iron, so one person sharpens another."

(PROVERBS 27:17)

Loneliness in an ungodly world can feel suffocating, as the emptiness deepens without the comfort of God's presence and true community. God didn't create you to walk this journey alone. He blesses you with friends and family to walk beside you, offering support, encouragement, and wisdom.

Just as iron sharpens iron, godly friendships refine you, helping you grow in faith and in Christlikeness.

These relationships are gifts from God, meant to challenge and encourage you and bring out the best in you. When you're facing struggles, they provide a listening ear and a prayerful heart. When you're rejoicing, they celebrate with you.

Take time today to appreciate the people God has placed in your life. Whether it's a close friend, a family member, or a fellow believer, remember that these relationships are divinely appointed to help you grow. Cherish them, and be intentional about nurturing these bonds. God uses others to strengthen, uplift, and sharpen you along your walk with Him.

A Prayer in Times of Anxiety

Lord, when loneliness wraps around me like a heavy cloak and anxiety tells me to isolate, remind me You created me for connection. Thank You for relationships that sharpen and refine me. When I'm tempted to withdraw, help me reach out instead. Thank You for people You've appointed to walk alongside me, listen, pray, and point me back to You when anxiety clouds my vision. Give me courage to be vulnerable. Help me both receive and give the blessing of true community that drives away loneliness. Amen.

STILLING THE STORM WITHIN

How has anxiety influenced your willingness to be vulnerable in relationships, and what might change if you allowed others to "sharpen" you?

Which relationship in your life has God used most powerfully to strengthen your faith during anxious seasons?

What step can you take today to nurture a relationship that God has placed in your life, even if anxiety makes connection feel difficult?

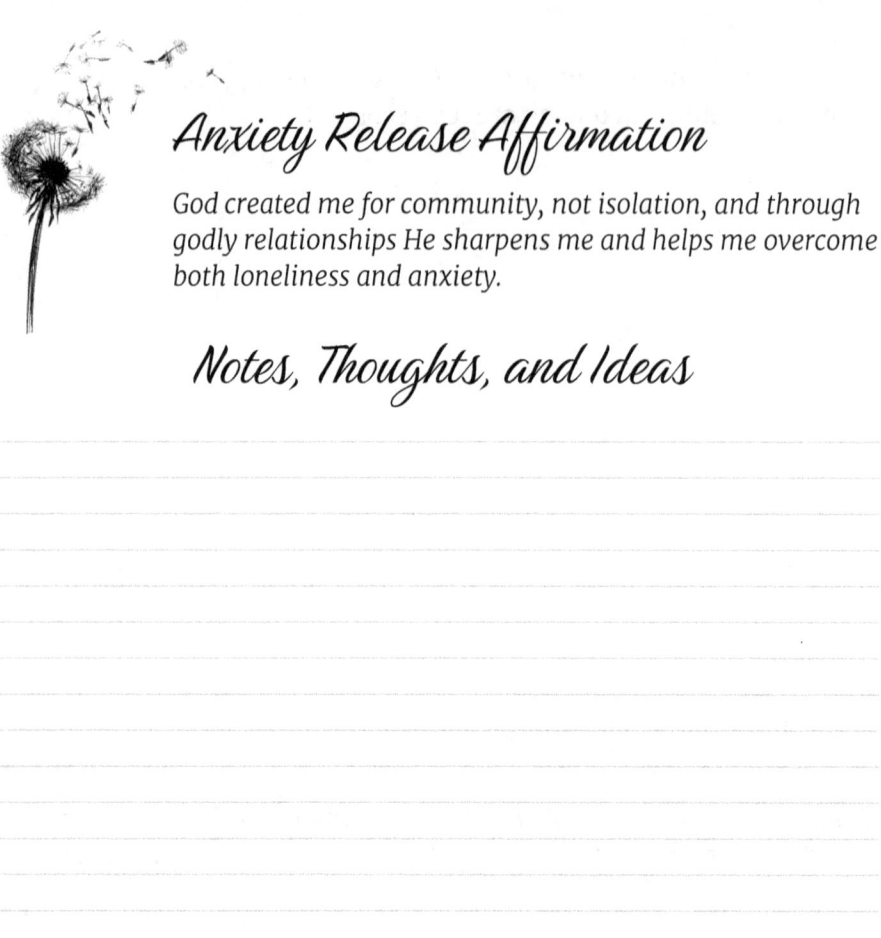

Anxiety Release Affirmation

God created me for community, not isolation, and through godly relationships He sharpens me and helps me overcome both loneliness and anxiety.

Notes, Thoughts, and Ideas

ENCOURAGEMENT FOR THE WEEK AHEAD

Anxiety often convinces us that isolation is safer than connection, that our struggles are too heavy for others to bear. But the very loneliness that intensifies our anxiety is what God designed relationships to heal. The friction of iron against iron isn't comfortable—vulnerability rarely is—but without it, both pieces remain dull. Your anxious heart wasn't meant to process life alone. The people God places in your path aren't coincidences; they're divine appointments. When you allow others to know your struggles, to pray with you, to walk alongside you, something beautiful happens: the weight becomes lighter, not because the burden changed, but because it's now carried by more than one set of shoulders.

Week 43: The Light in Laughter

*"A happy heart makes the face cheerful,
but heartache crushes the spirit."*

(PROVERBS 15:13)

Do you recall the last time when you were laughing so hard you couldn't catch your breath? This is the laughter that bubbles up from within, filling your heart and soul with a joy so deep it takes your breath away. There's more to this than just fun!

When God blesses you with moments of laughter, it's not just fun—it's a gift of renewal. These joyful times are gifts from God, reminders of His goodness and love. He wants you to experience not just quiet peace but also the exuberant, carefree joy that makes you laugh until you can't catch your breath. In those moments, you feel light, free, and connected to Him and others in ways that strengthen your spirit.

Laughter lightens your heart, refreshes your spirit, and gives you the strength to carry on. In those joyful moments, God restores your energy and reminds you of His goodness. So, embrace these times of laughter, knowing they're a reminder that God is sustaining you and filling you with renewed strength to let your spirit soar.

A Prayer in Times of Anxiety

God of joy and laughter, thank You for belly laughs that make my sides ache and tears stream down my face. In times of overwhelming worry, remind me of moments when joy bubbled up and couldn't coexist with wonder. Thank You for designing laughter as medicine for my soul. When fears tempt me to take everything too seriously, help me remember how to laugh freely again. Restore to me the joy of Your salvation that lifts my spirits and lightens my load. Amen.

STILLING THE STORM WITHIN

When was the last time you experienced deep, soul-refreshing laughter, and how did it affect your anxiety in that moment?

_____
_____
_____
_____
_____
_____
_____
_____
_____
_____
_____
_____
_____
_____
_____
_____

How might intentionally seeking moments of joy and laughter change your approach to managing anxiety?

What people or situations most consistently bring laughter into your life, and how can you prioritize these connections?

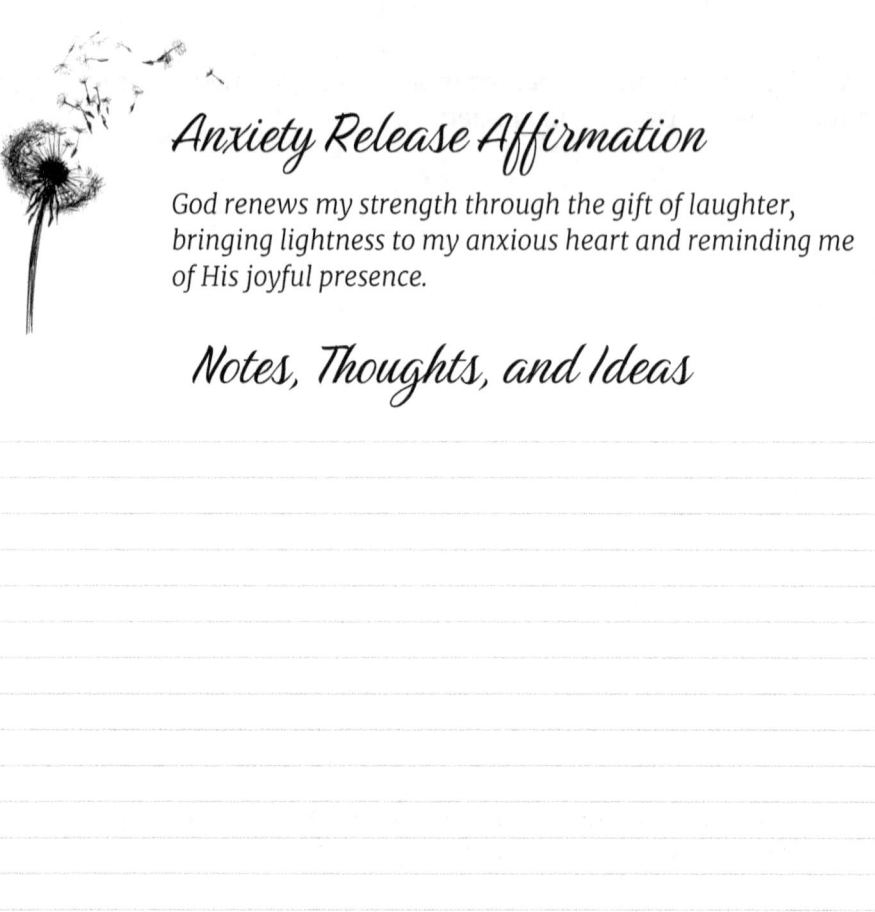

Anxiety Release Affirmation

God renews my strength through the gift of laughter, bringing lightness to my anxious heart and reminding me of His joyful presence.

Notes, Thoughts, and Ideas

ENCOURAGEMENT FOR THE WEEK AHEAD

Anxiety has a way of making everything feel heavy—conversations, decisions, even breathing itself. It convinces us that seriousness equals control. But God, in His wisdom, gave us laughter as a relief valve for our overpressured souls. Those moments when joy overtakes you completely aren't just pleasant interruptions; they're holy spaces where healing happens. The lightness you feel when laughter bubbles up is your spirit remembering its true nature—not weighed down by worry but lifted by love. Don't dismiss these moments as merely recreational. They are restorative, rebuilding what anxiety tears down. Make room for laughter today. It's not frivolous—it's faithful. It's not just fun—it's freedom.

Week 44: Do Life Together

"Two are better than one, because they have a good return for their labor: If either of them falls down, one can help the other up. But pity anyone who falls and has no one to help them up."

(ECCLESIASTES 4:9-10)

Loneliness often stems from feeling disconnected, misunderstood, or unseen, leaving a longing for meaningful connection that the world can't satisfy. God never intended for you to walk through life alone. He blesses you with kindred spirits—friends, family, and fellow believers—to share the journey. These relationships are His design, meant to lift you when you stumble, encourage you when you're weary, and celebrate with you in moments of joy.

Godly people are a precious gift. They challenge you to grow, help you stay grounded in faith, and remind you of God's love when the world feels overwhelming. Life becomes richer when shared with others who are walking with God and encouraging you in His truth.

So, embrace the people God has placed in your life. Seek out those relationships, invest in them, and allow others to support and uplift you. Together, you can strengthen each other and experience God's love more deeply. You don't have to do life alone.

A Prayer in Times of Anxiety

Father, when loneliness and anxiety make me feel unseen, remind me You created me for community. Thank You for the kindred spirits in my life. When anxiety tempts me to withdraw, give me courage to reach out. Thank You for friends who understand, family who stand by me, and believers who point me to Your truth. Help me receive support through others and invest in relationships that calm my anxious spirit. Amen.

STILLING THE STORM WITHIN

How has anxiety affected your ability to maintain meaningful connections, and what might change if you viewed relationships as God's design for healing?

Who has God placed in your life that helps you feel less alone in your struggles with worry and fear?

What practical step can you take this week to deepen a relationship that strengthens your faith and calms your anxious thoughts?

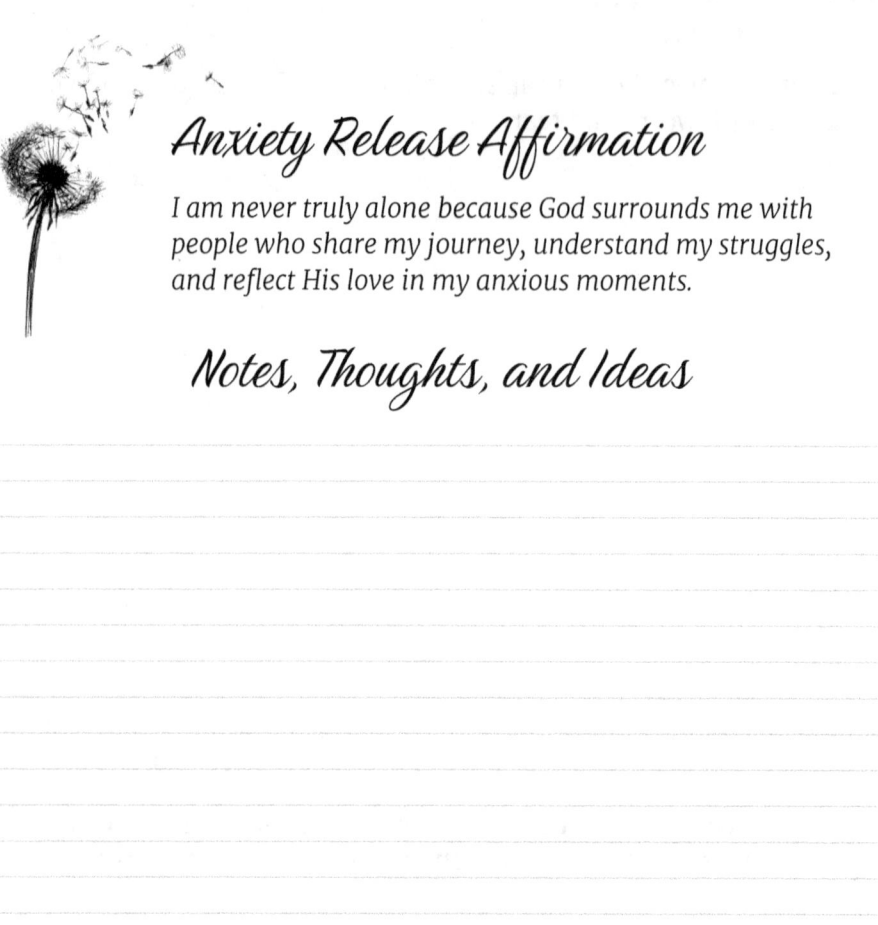

Anxiety Release Affirmation

I am never truly alone because God surrounds me with people who share my journey, understand my struggles, and reflect His love in my anxious moments.

Notes, Thoughts, and Ideas

ENCOURAGEMENT FOR THE WEEK AHEAD

Anxiety often whispers that we're better off alone—that vulnerability is dangerous and isolation is safer than risking misunderstanding. But God's design tells a different story. The very connections we avoid when anxiety rises are often the ones that would help it subside. When you feel overwhelmed by worry, reaching out rather than retreating can be the bravest act of faith. Those godly friends who know your struggles without judgment, who pray when you can't find the words, who sit with you in the darkness—they're not just nice additions to your life. They're essential threads in God's tapestry of care for you. Today, remember that community isn't just comforting—it's healing. You were made to be known, loved, and supported through every season.

Week 45: In the Cheerleader's Presence

*"A cheerful heart is good medicine,
but a crushed spirit dries up the bones."*

(PROVERBS 17:22)

You know the constant weight that never quite lifts. This is the reality of anxiety that preoccupies the mind. It's hard to feel cheerful when your mind is filled with worry, and it can seem impossible to cultivate joy. It's easier to dwell over a crushed spirit. But God understands your struggle and offers a comforting truth—He desires to heal your heart and cheer you up, even in anxious moments.

A cheerful heart doesn't mean ignoring your struggles or pretending everything is fine. It's a heart that chooses to trust God, despite the uncertainty. When you bring your worries to Him, you consciously prevent your spirit from being crushed. He replaces anxiety with His peace, offering you moments of joy that refresh your soul. Even in the midst of your anxiety, God invites you to experience the healing power of a cheerful heart—a heart that finds strength in His love.

You can live the miracle of keeping the cheerfulness of heart, even in the presence of worries!

A Prayer in Times of Anxiety

Father, when anxiety weighs on my chest and worry fills my mind, I confess how hard it is to feel cheerful. Thank You for understanding and not just telling me to "cheer up." When anxious thoughts crush my spirit, help me bring my worries to You instead of dwelling on them alone. Thank You for wanting to replace my anxiety with peace. Teach me to find joy not by ignoring reality, but by trusting You within it. Help me experience the miracle of cheerfulness even amid worry. Amen.

STILLING THE STORM WITHIN

When anxiety feels overwhelming, what small sources of joy could you intentionally focus on to begin lifting your crushed spirit?

How does bringing your worries to God, rather than dwelling on them alone, affect your ability to maintain a cheerful heart?

What practice could help you choose faith over fear and anxiety when your mind starts spiraling with worry?

Anxiety Release Affirmation

God desires to heal my anxious heart with His joy, and I can experience the miracle of cheerfulness even while acknowledging my struggles.

Notes, Thoughts, and Ideas

ENCOURAGEMENT FOR THE WEEK AHEAD

Anxiety and joy often feel like opposing forces that cannot coexist. But what if they're not mutually exclusive? What if the cheerful heart God promises isn't about the absence of worries but about His presence among them? The miracle isn't that your anxieties magically disappear—it's that they don't get the final word on your spirit. When worry threatens to crush you, bringing those concerns to God creates space for something else to grow alongside them: trust, hope, even moments of unexpected joy. This isn't about forcing happiness or pretending everything's fine. It's about allowing God to plant seeds of cheerfulness in the very soil of your anxious thoughts. Today, your spirit doesn't have to be crushed by what weighs on you. Choose to bring it to Him instead.

Week 46: The Reason to Trust

"Trust in Him at all times, O people; pour out your heart before Him; God is a refuge for us."

(PSALM 62:8)

Trusting can be hard, especially if you've been hurt or let down in the past. It's easy to feel like you can't fully rely on anyone. But God is different. Again and again, He has proved Himself true and faithful. He is your safe place—a home where your heart can find peace, no matter how many walls you've built up.

God invites you to bring your doubts, fears, and pain to Him. He isn't like people who might disappoint you; He is unwavering in His love for you.

When the world feels unpredictable, He remains your refuge, a place where you can always find rest and protection. When you pour out your heart, He embraces you to assure you, and He moves on your behalf to help you.

So, even when trust feels difficult, remember that God is trustworthy at all times. Pour out your heart to Him, knowing He is the solid foundation that will never fail you.

A Prayer in Times of Anxiety

Father, when anxiety makes trust feel impossible and past hurts have built walls around my heart, draw me to Your faithfulness. Thank You for being different from those who let me down—a safe place where my guarded heart can rest. When doubt overwhelms me, help me remember how You've proven Yourself true. Give me courage to pour out my heart completely. Thank You for embracing my vulnerability. When the world feels chaotic, remind me You remain my unwavering refuge. Help me lean into Your trustworthiness today. Amen.

STILLING THE STORM WITHIN

What specific moments of disappointment have shaped your hesitation to trust, and how might God be inviting you to heal from them?

What evidence of God's faithfulness in your past can serve as an anchor when anxiety tempts you to doubt Him now?

What specific fears or worries are you holding back from pouring out to God, and what might change if you fully trusted Him with them?

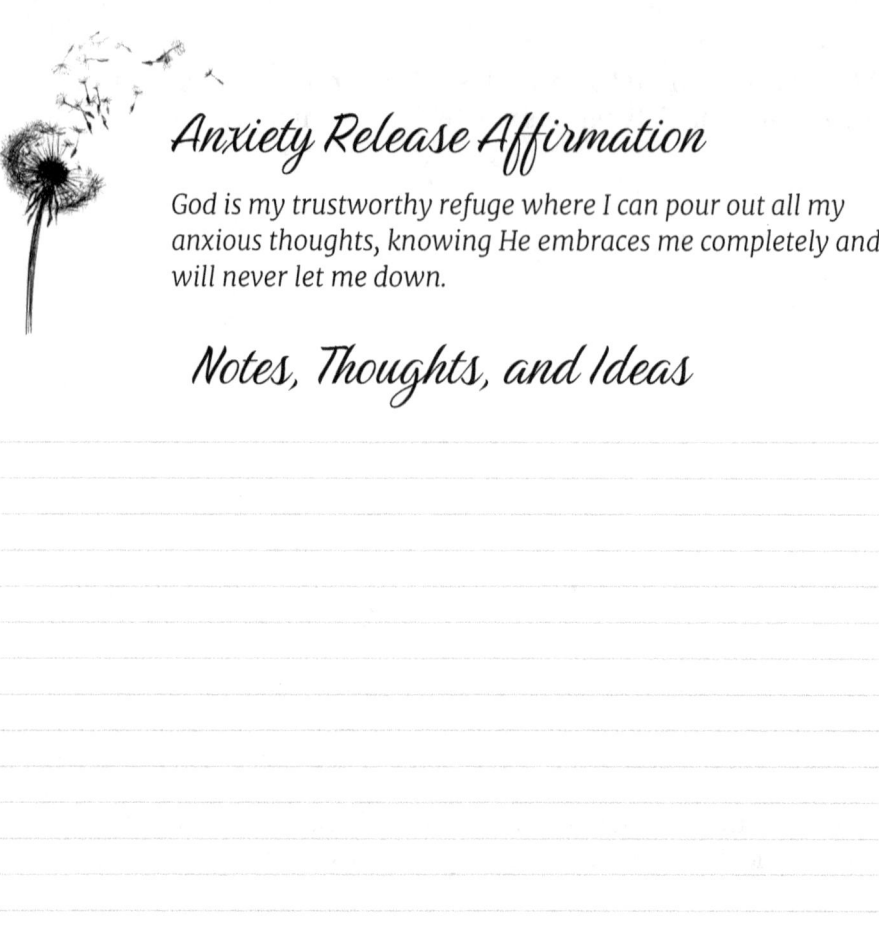

Anxiety Release Affirmation

God is my trustworthy refuge where I can pour out all my anxious thoughts, knowing He embraces me completely and will never let me down.

Notes, Thoughts, and Ideas

ENCOURAGEMENT FOR THE WEEK AHEAD

Trust is rebuilt in small moments of surrender—each time you choose to lower your defenses and pour out another worry to God. Anxiety often feeds on our reluctance to fully trust, convincing us that keeping our fears close protects us somehow. But the walls we build to keep disappointment out also keep peace at bay. Today, consider what it might feel like to truly pour out your heart without reservation, to bring every anxious thought to the One who already knows them all. Not because He demands your vulnerability, but because He designed you for it. In His presence, your guarded heart can finally exhale. The God who has proven Himself faithful through generations stands ready to prove Himself faithful to you again.

Week 47: Life-Giving Love

"My soul is overwhelmed with sorrow to the point of death"

(MATTHEW 26:38)

There is grief that is unbearable, even if it is grieving about your anxiety. It feels physically and emotionally life-draining, as if the weight of pain could lead you to eternal anguish, leaving no relief.

Jesus, fully God and fully man, understood the depths of human suffering. In His moment of anguish, just before His arrest and crucifixion, He didn't hide His pain. He was honest about His sorrow, admitting it was so deep it felt like death itself.

This is such a powerful reminder for you today. Jesus, who walked through the darkest moments, invites you to bring your own pain to God with the same honesty. You can expose yourself with Him and still be loved. It's okay to feel overwhelmed, to experience sorrow and anguish, and to express it to God. He understands and doesn't shy away from your deepest struggles.

In doing so, you draw closer to Him, finding comfort, strength, and the reassurance that He's with you. Then you realize how truly constant His love is for you and how enlivening it is.

A Prayer in Times of Anxiety

Lord Jesus, when grief feels unbearable and anxiety weighs heavily, thank You for understanding this pain firsthand. When my sorrow is too deep for words, remind me that You too experienced such anguish. Thank You for showing me I can be honest without rejection. When anxiety and grief drain life from me, help me remember You invite my raw emotions. Thank You for not turning away but drawing close. Comfort me knowing You're with me in this valley, Your love constant and Your presence life-giving. Amen.

STILLING THE STORM WITHIN

How does knowing that Jesus experienced overwhelming sorrow change how you view your own grief and anxiety?

When grief and anxiety feel unbearable, what practice helps you most in remembering God's constant presence with you?

In what ways has anxiety amplified your grief, and how does Jesus's example offer a different way to carry both?

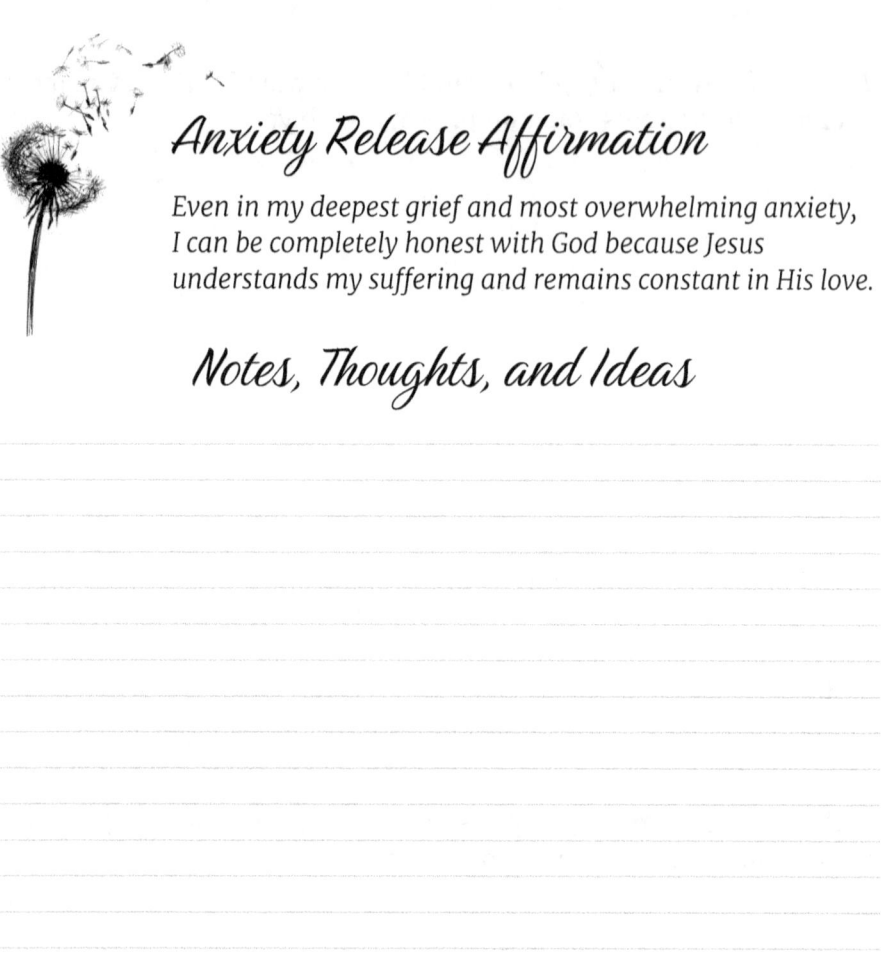

Anxiety Release Affirmation

Even in my deepest grief and most overwhelming anxiety, I can be completely honest with God because Jesus understands my suffering and remains constant in His love.

Notes, Thoughts, and Ideas

ENCOURAGEMENT FOR THE WEEK AHEAD

There's something sacred about acknowledging unbearable pain—about admitting when grief and anxiety have drained us beyond what we thought possible to endure. In those moments when breathing feels like an act of courage, remember that Jesus himself knew this territory. He didn't spiritualize his anguish or minimize it. He named it honestly: "My soul is overwhelmed with sorrow to the point of death." His vulnerability creates space for yours. You don't need to pretend your burden is lighter than it is or that your faith makes you immune to suffering. The Savior who knelt in Gethsemane understands the weight you carry. And in that understanding, something miraculous happens—not the immediate lifting of grief perhaps, but the profound comfort of being fully known and still completely loved.

Week 48: Boasting of the Weak

*"My grace is sufficient for you,
for my power is made perfect in weakness."*

(2 CORINTHIANS 12:9)

It's hard to feel strong when you're facing personal struggles, weaknesses, or limitations. It's easy to want to hide those parts of yourself or feel defeated by them. It's also how you are accused by the enemy that you are faithless. But God wants you to know that in your weakness, His power shines brightest.

While you are finite, He is infinite.

His grace is sufficient—not just enough, but abundantly enough for whatever you're facing. In those moments when you feel least capable, His strength is at work within you. You don't need to have it all together; God's power is displayed when you're honest about your need for Him. It will be a majestic work in your life!

He never condemns you for your limitations. So, embrace your weaknesses, knowing that they are opportunities for His grace to shine through. His power, in your vulnerability, is more than enough.

A Prayer in Times of Anxiety

Father, when anxiety makes me feel weak and accused of faithlessness, help me remember Your power shines in my limitations. When I feel inadequate, thank You that Your grace is abundantly enough. Remind me my weaknesses are opportunities for Your strength to display. Thank You for not condemning my limitations but meeting me with infinite power where I am most finite. Help me embrace vulnerability today, trusting Your grace will shine through every broken place in my life. Amen.

STILLING THE STORM WITHIN

How does the enemy use your anxiety to make you feel faithless, and what truth from God counters those accusations?

What weaknesses or limitations do you try hardest to hide, and how might God want to display His power through them?

What would it look like to truly embrace your vulnerability as an opportunity for God's grace rather than viewing it as something to overcome?

Anxiety Release Affirmation

God's power is made perfect in my weakness, and His abundant grace transforms my anxiety and limitations into displays of His strength.

Notes, Thoughts, and Ideas

ENCOURAGEMENT FOR THE WEEK AHEAD

Anxiety often feels like the ultimate evidence of our weakness—proof that we're not strong enough, faithful enough, or trusting enough. But what if these very places of vulnerability are precisely where God does His most majestic work? The parts of yourself you most want to hide may be the very windows through which His light shines most clearly. Your limitations aren't failures to overcome but invitations to experience grace in its purest form. Today, resist the urge to appear stronger than you are. Instead, bring your trembling heart, your racing thoughts, and your overwhelming fears straight to the One whose infinite strength steps into your story just as it is—no edits required. Your weakness isn't your shame; it's your invitation to witness God's power in action.

Week 49: Community of Love

"Carry each other's burdens."

(GALATIANS 6:2)

When there's too much to carry, the tendency to isolate creeps in, convincing you that distance will make life easier, but it deepens loneliness and worsens your misery.

God has blessed you with a beautiful gift—community.

When you share your pain and struggles, you allow others to step in and offer their strength, prayer, and love. And in return, you're also called to do the same for them.

When you open up and allow others to help carry your burdens, you not only experience God's love more deeply, but you also reflect the heart of Jesus. Through selfless acts of support, we fulfill the law of Christ, which is to love one another as He has loved us.

So, don't hesitate to reach out when you need help, and be willing to offer your own support. You can walk this path alongside others, lifting each other in love and fulfilling God's purpose for His people.

A Prayer in Times of Anxiety

Lord, when anxiety tells me isolation is safer than connection, remind me of community's gift. When burdens feel too heavy, give me courage to reach out. Thank You for people who help carry my load. Forgive me for choosing loneliness over vulnerability. Help me trust others with my struggles and carry theirs in return. Thank You for showing Your love through those around me. Help me reflect Jesus by giving and receiving support in anxious seasons. Amen.

STILLING THE STORM WITHIN

When anxiety tempts you to isolate, what specific fears are driving that tendency to withdraw?

How has God used others to lighten your burdens in the past, and what did that teach you about community?

What prevents you from allowing others to help carry your anxiety, and how might overcoming that resistance fulfill God's design for community?

Anxiety Release Affirmation

God has blessed me with community to share my burdens, and through both giving and receiving support,
I fulfill Christ's law of love.

Notes, Thoughts, and Ideas

ENCOURAGEMENT FOR THE WEEK AHEAD

Anxiety whispers that vulnerability is dangerous and that we should handle our struggles alone. But isolation only amplifies our fears, making the weight feel even heavier than before. The community God provides isn't just a nice addition to our faith—it's an essential expression of it. When we allow others to see our struggles and help carry our burdens, we experience the tangible love of Christ. And remarkably, in those moments of shared weight, something beautiful happens—the burden becomes lighter for everyone. Today, resist the urge to pull away when anxiety rises. Instead, take the brave step of reaching out. Your willingness to be honest about your needs isn't weakness; it's an invitation for others to fulfill their calling and for you to experience God's love in human form.

Week 50: Tunneling Together

*"But if we walk in the light, as he is in the light,
we have fellowship with one another,
and the blood of Jesus, his Son, purifies us from all sin."*

(1 JOHN 1:7)

Groping in the darkness of anxiety feels disorienting and frightening, as if every step is uncertain, with no light ahead. This becomes even more intense when you're alone.

As God's children, you are called to walk in His light together. The journey of faith can often feel like walking through a dark tunnel, but you're never meant to walk it alone. God has placed fellow believers around you to help illuminate the way.

In a community, you can be encouraged as you share your struggles and be helped to grow in Godliness. With a community of faith, your life reflects God's light, overcoming darkness and sin. The light of Christ purifies you and enables you to live in a way that honors Him and builds others up.

So, don't isolate yourself. Embrace the community of believers God has given you. Together, you can light the way and overcome any challenge through godliness and grace.

A Prayer in Times of Anxiety

Father, when anxiety surrounds me like darkness making each step uncertain, thank You for not leaving me alone. When isolation tempts me to withdraw, remind me You've called me to walk in Your light with others. Thank You for community that illuminates my path. Help me resist hiding my struggles. Give me courage to step into fellowship and be vulnerable about my anxieties. Thank You that in community, Your light overcomes darkness and Your grace carries me through. Amen.

STILLING THE STORM WITHIN

How has anxiety created darkness in your life, and what would it look like to allow God's light through community to illuminate those spaces?

How might your perspective on anxiety shift if you viewed it not as a personal failure but as an opportunity for connection?

What specific fear keeps you from being honest about your anxiety with your community of faith?

Anxiety Release Affirmation

I am called to walk in God's light together with others, where my anxiety loses power and His purifying presence transforms my darkness.

Notes, Thoughts, and Ideas

ENCOURAGEMENT FOR THE WEEK AHEAD

Anxiety thrives in isolation, growing stronger in the darkness of our aloneness. Each uncertain step feels more treacherous when there's no one beside us holding up a light. But God's design offers a powerful alternative—a community of believers who illuminate the path together. When one person's light flickers under the weight of fear, others can shine more brightly until that season passes. Your anxiety doesn't disqualify you from this fellowship; it might actually be why you need it most. Today, resist the pull toward isolation. Take one small step toward the light of community, allowing others to see your struggles and help guide you through them. The darkness may not immediately disappear, but in the warm glow of shared faith, it loses its power to terrify.

Week 51: Blessed Hopefulness

"He gives strength to the weary and increases the power of the weak. Even youths grow tired and weary, and young men stumble and fall; but those who hope in the Lord will renew their strength. They will soar on wings like eagles; they will run and not grow weary, they will walk and not be faint."

(ISAIAH 40:29-31)

Life can knock you flat sometimes, even in your so-called "prime." The stress and anxiety sneak up on you. One day you're fine; the next you're drowning in responsibilities. And somewhere in that mess, you forgot about you. Your battery warning light is flashing red.

The constant juggling act leaves you hollow-eyed at midnight, wondering how you'll face tomorrow. Some days, just making breakfast feels like climbing Everest. You're not broken. You're human.

God is the source of strength when yours runs low.

No matter how worn out or overwhelmed you feel, He promises to renew your energy. He doesn't expect you to power through on your own; He invites you to lean into Him. Through the ups and downs of life, God will give you the strength you need to keep going, and He will lift you when you feel like you can't take another step.

A Prayer in Times of Anxiety

God, when life knocks me flat and anxiety sneaks up unexpectedly, when I feel completely depleted, I come to You. When responsibilities pile high and simple tasks feel overwhelming, thank You that I don't have to power through alone. When I'm wide awake at midnight wondering about tomorrow, remind me You are the source that never runs dry.
Help me hope in You today, especially when burnout tempts me to despair. Lift me up when I can't take another step. Amen.

STILLING THE STORM WITHIN

When have you recently tried to power through on your own strength rather than leaning into God's renewable energy?

What specific responsibilities or pressures are currently depleting you, and how might surrendering them to God change your experience?

How does your anxiety increase when you forget that being human means having limitations?

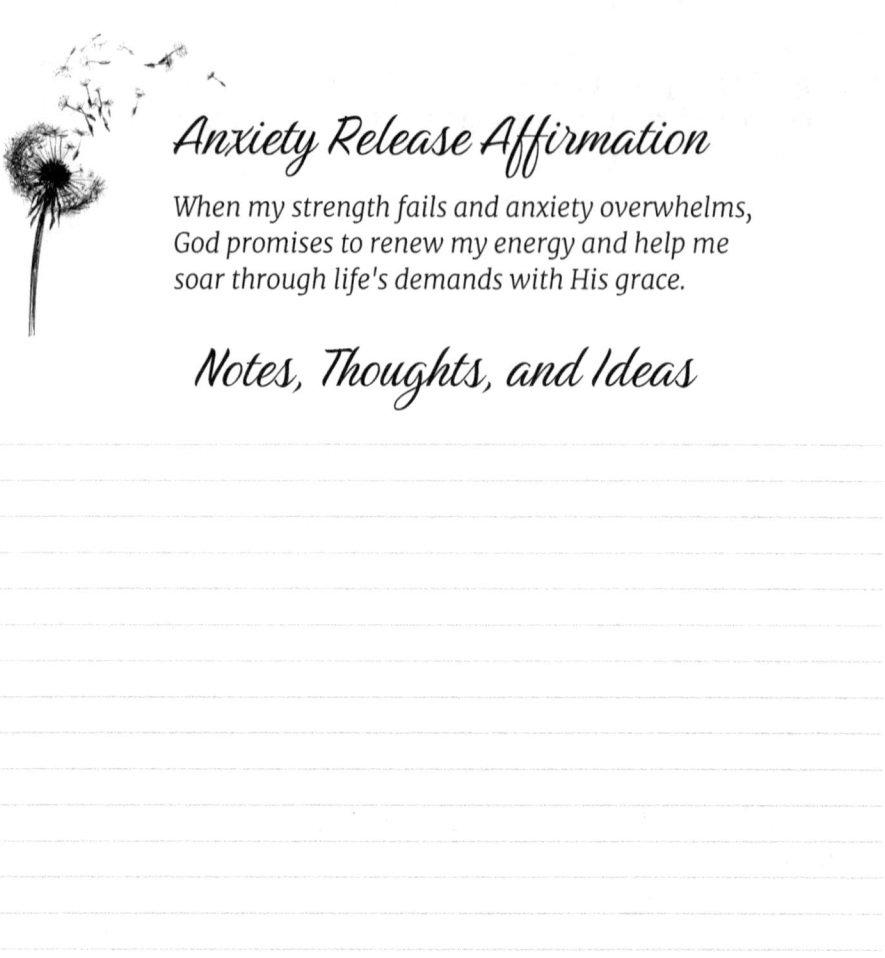

Anxiety Release Affirmation

When my strength fails and anxiety overwhelms, God promises to renew my energy and help me soar through life's demands with His grace.

Notes, Thoughts, and Ideas

ENCOURAGEMENT FOR THE WEEK AHEAD

There's something powerful about admitting we're at the end of ourselves. That moment—when we finally acknowledge our battery is completely drained—isn't actually failure. It's the precise point where genuine renewal becomes possible. Anxiety often stems from trying to be superhuman in a world that demands everything and offers little rest in return. But God never designed you to run indefinitely without recharging. The beauty of faith isn't that it makes you invincible; it's that it connects you to an eternal power source when your own strength inevitably runs out. Today, you don't have to climb your personal Everest alone. You don't have to pretend you're fine when you're not. Your admission of weariness isn't weakness—it's the first step toward the strength that soars.

Week 52: The Healer's Heart

*"The Lord is close to the brokenhearted
and saves those who are crushed in spirit."*

(PSALM 34:18)

In times of pain, it's easy to feel like you need to hide your hurt or put on a brave face. But God invites you to come as you are—raw, vulnerable, and real. There's no need to muster any strength and to pretend you're OK when you're in His presence.

He sees your heart exactly as it is, and He loves you fully, without judgment. God doesn't expect you to have it all together; He just wants you to bring your brokenness to Him.

In this covenant relationship, He's not distant or aloof. He's close to the brokenhearted, offering comfort and healing in the midst of your struggles. And He alone can mend your heart. You realize the pieces are coming together the more you draw near to God.

So, don't be afraid to be honest with God. He is a safe place where you can express your deepest pain and find the love, peace, and restoration you need.

A Prayer in Times of Anxiety

Lord, when anxiety makes me hide behind masks, remind me that You invite me to come exactly as I am. Thank You that with You, I don't need to pretend I'm okay or muster strength I don't have. When my heart feels shattered, thank You for drawing near. I'm grateful You see every broken piece and love me completely without judgment. Help me trust You enough to be honest about my pain and fears. Thank You for being my safe place, where vulnerability is met with healing comfort. Teach me to bring my anxiety to You first, without filtering it. Amen.

STILLING THE STORM WITHIN

How might your experience of anxiety change if you stopped trying to "have it all together" before coming to God?

What parts of your heart have you been afraid to show God, and what might happen if you allowed Him to see those places?

When you think about being completely honest with God about your fears and worries, what holds you back from that level of vulnerability?

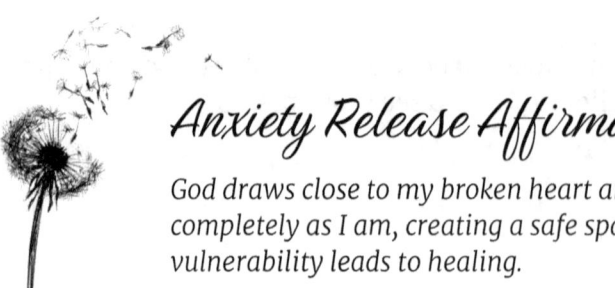

Anxiety Release Affirmation

God draws close to my broken heart and loves me completely as I am, creating a safe space where my honest vulnerability leads to healing.

Notes, Thoughts, and Ideas

ENCOURAGEMENT FOR THE WEEK AHEAD

Anxiety often thrives in the gap between who we are and who we think we should be. We exhaust ourselves trying to appear strong, put-together, and faithfully untroubled. But what if the path to healing isn't through perfecting our spiritual performance but through embracing our imperfection before God? The invitation to come as you are isn't just permission to be honest—it's an essential requirement for genuine restoration. Your broken places aren't shameful secrets to hide; they're sacred spaces where God's presence becomes most real. Today, set down the exhausting work of pretending. Let your masks fall away. The God who sees you completely loves you completely, and in His gentle presence, the pieces of your heart begin finding their way back together.

Thank you for reading

I hope you loved this devotional as much as I enjoyed writing it. These devotions came from my heart to yours, and I cherish knowing how they've touched your life.

I truly appreciate your support and the time you've taken to read this book. If you feel called to, please leave a review so other anxious Christians can find the help they need. Your words of love also help me as an author to inspire as many people as I can. Reviews don't have to be long—even a few sentences sharing your experience with the book make a big difference!

You can leave your review here: http://links.wingsofgracepublishing.com/anxiety-devotional or use the QR code below:

What's Next?

Congratulations on completing this devotional experience! The prayers, reflections, and Scripture passages you've engaged with over these weeks have begun a meaningful transformation in your relationship with anxiety and with God.

If this devotional has resonated with you, I invite you to explore *"From Worry to Worship: God's Path to Living Free from Anxiety, Worry, and Stress."* While this devotional has given you weekly touch points for reflection and prayer, the main book offers a deeper exploration of the biblical foundations for anxiety management and faith-based strategies for lasting peace.

The book expands on many of the themes you've encountered here.

Join My Book Launch Team

Want to be part of something special?

I'm looking for amazing readers to join my book launch team. As a team member, you'll get early access to new books and devotionals, behind-the-scenes updates, and the chance to help spread the word about books that matter.

It's simple, fun, and it would be such a blessing to have you as part of the process. If you want to help my books and devotionals reach more hearts, I'd love to have you on the team.

Head to **https://wingsofgracepublishing.com/join/** to learn more and join us!

About the Author

Grace Andrews is a Christian author passionate about sharing the transformative power of faith through inspirational writing. With a heart for spiritual growth, she offers readers practical insights and biblical wisdom to help them navigate life's challenges.

She is fueled by coffee and the love of her husband of 25 years. She adores international travel, quiet moments with God, reading, and creating. Grace both writes and designs all of her own books, including the covers and interior layout.

Grace believes that God's love and guidance can lead anyone to greater peace, purpose, and fulfillment.

Find out more about Grace and her books here:

https://wingsofgracepublishing.com/

Turn Worry into Worship with This Guide

As a thank you for purchasing this devotional, I want to offer you the *'Hand Your Anxiety Over to God'* Surrender Plan. This simple, free guide will help you stop spiraling thoughts, find peace in His presence, and turn worry into worship.

I'd also love to gift you my 7-day mini-course on trusting and living in God's grace. It will automatically be delivered, along with the guide.

Download the guide here:

https://wingsofgracepublishing.com/surrender/

or use the QR code below:

www.ingramcontent.com/pod-product-compliance
Lightning Source LLC
Chambersburg PA
CBHW072000070526
44583CB00015B/1276